Amazonia

THE LAND, THE WILDLIFE, THE RIVER, THE PEOPLE

Afonso Capelas Jr.

FIREFLY BOOKS

A FIREFLY BOOK

Published by Firefly Books Ltd. 2003

National Library of Canada Cataloguing in Publication Data

Capelas, Afonso
        Amazonia : the land, the wildlife, the river, the people /
Afonso Capelas, Jr.

Includes bibliographical references and index.
ISBN 1-55297-589-4

        1. Amazon River Region. 2. Amazon River. 3. Natural
history-Amazon River Region. 4. Rain forest ecology-Amazon River
Region. 5. Watershed ecology-Amazon River Watershed. I. Title.

QH112.C36 2003   508.81'1   C2003-900397-3

Published in Canada in 2003 by Firefly Books Ltd.
3680 Victoria Park Avenua
Toronto, Ontario
M2H 3K1

First published in 2003 in New Zealand by David Bateman Ltd.,
30 Tarndale Grove,
Albany, Auckland,
New Zealand

Page 2: The Caciporé River winds through the rainforest for over 185 miles (300 km).
Page 3: The *jacarés açu* or black caiman.
Page 4: Still waters and sunshine on a river channel in Amazonia.
Opposite: Brilliantly-colored macaws are just one of many striking Amazonian birds.
Pages 8–9: The huge lily pads of the Amazonian water lily (*Victoria amazonica*).
Page 10: Rainbows are a common sight over the rainforest, as clouds gather for the daily downpour.

Publisher Cataloging-in-Publication Data (U.S.)
(Library of Congress Standards)

Capelas, Afonso.
        Amazonia : the land, the wildlife, the river, the people /
Afonso Capelas. –1st ed.
 [150] p. : col. photos. ; cm.
Includes bibliographical references and index.
Summary: Comprehensive and panoramic reference on one of the mightiest
and most diverse ecosystems on Earth
ISBN 1-55297-589-4
1. Ecology--Amazon River Region. 2. Rain forest ecology-Amazon River
Region.   3. Natural resources-Amazon River Valley. 4. Amazon River
Region. I. Title.
333.75/ 0981/1 21   QH112.C374 2003

Published in the United States in 2003 by Firefly Books (U.S.) Inc.
P.O. Box 1338, Ellicott Station
Buffalo, New York
14205

Text: Edward Horton, based on the original text by Afonso Capelas Jr. and Alexandra Gonzales
Photography: Reflexo
Printed in China through Colorcraft Ltd.

Amazonia

Contents

AMAZON BASIN

CHAPTER ONE
History

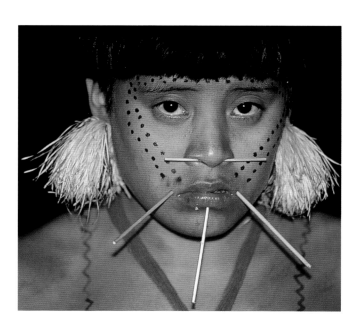

Amazonia—a legendary land

The earliest inhabitants of Amazonia probably arrived some 10,000 to 15,000 years ago, following the great migration across the Bering Strait that first peopled the Americas. At that time, towards the end of the most recent Ice Age, the sea level was perhaps 100 feet (30 m) lower than it is today because so much of the world's water was locked up in ice. This exposed a very broad land bridge between Siberia and Alaska, and nomadic hunters from central Asia trailed their prey as mastadons, hairy mammoths and other species made their way across. These first American immigrants then spread throughout the entire New World, and became the ancestors of all native peoples from the Inuit and Aleut of the Arctic to the Tehuelche of Patagonia. Until the closing years of the 15th century the Americas were theirs alone.

When Christopher Columbus dropped anchor off the coast of San Salvador in October 1492 it marked the end of America's isolation from the rest of the world, and the beginning of what is known as the European age — the time when European nations expanded their power and influence all around the globe. The first glimpse Amazonia had of the turbulent time ahead came in 1541. By then, Spanish conquistadors led by the redoubtable Francisco Pizarro had destroyed the mighty Inca empire in Peru and Ecuador, and Pizarro's younger brother Gonzalo Pizarro mounted an expedition from

Opposite: Yanomami children.
Pages 12–13: The Xikrin people, now living in the Xingu Indigenous Park in southeastern Brazil.
Page 13: Yanomami woman in ceremonial dress.

Above: The Jaú River, in the Rio Negro basin. Close by is Jaú National Park, the largest national park in Brazil, which received World Heritage Site status in 2000.

Opposite: The children of the Yanomami people who live in northern Amazonia, around the border of Brazil and Venezuela.

Quito in Ecuador to explore the South American interior. After crossing the Andes, the expedition got bogged down on the banks of the Upper Napo. With supplies nearly exhausted, Pizarro decided that salvation lay in searching further inland for food. A boat was built and about 60 of the original 280 conquistadors set off downstream, under the command of Francisco Orellana. They never returned, leaving Pizarro and the others to struggle back to Quito. Meanwhile, Orellana and his men survived a number of brushes with hostile natives as they successfully navigated the entire length of the Amazon river system, sailing out into the Atlantic 16 months later.

To the earliest European explorers Amazonia was a land of legendary female warriors and fabulous treasure. Orellana's epic journey through what he dismissed as a "green hell" failed to dispel one persistent legend about Amazonia and planted another. The expedition had not been undertaken simply for the sake of adventure but to locate El Dorado, the "Gilded Man," a tribal chieftain of such fabled wealth that he was anointed with gold dust every day. El Dorado proved as elusive in 1541 as he and the fabled land that bears his name have been ever since. Orellana did, however, claim to have come across a race of awesome female warriors. They too have eluded all subsequent search parties, but have gained immortality through the name the Spanish gave them, and eventually the river and the entire region. It was inspired by the Greek myth of female archers who cut off their right breasts to improve their shooting technique: the legendary Amazons.

The Portuguese stake their claim

While it was the Spanish who made the first descent of the Amazon to its mouth, it was the Portuguese who eventually claimed the lion's share of Amazonia. This was largely fortuitous, a result of a famous papal bull promulgated by Pope Alexander VI in 1493 and, with modifications, enshrined in the Treaty of Tordesillas the following year. The pope grandly apportioned the whole of the unexplored regions of the world between the two Catholic powers, Spain and Portugal. An arbitrary line was drawn through the Atlantic from pole to pole. Everything to the east belonged to Portugal (giving it Africa, whose west coast the Portuguese had been busily exploring), everything to the west was Spain's (the Genoese-born Columbus had sailed in the service of Spain). The unintended effect of this was to give the eastern bulge of South America, as yet unsighted by

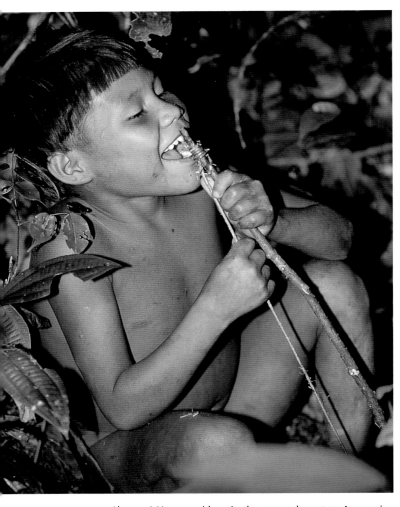

Above: A Yanomami boy. As the encroachment on Amazonia increases, nobody knows what will be the ultimate fate of its indigenous peoples.

Opposite: Sunset over the Amazon River.

European explorers, to Portugal. Over the next couple of centuries, the Portuguese spread up river from the mouth of Amazon to claim possession of what is now Brazil and the heart of Amazonia. In 1616, Francisco Branco built a fort at Presépio on the place where Belém, the state capital of Pará, stands today.

Two great expeditions were instrumental in the Portuguese push into the interior of the country. In 1637, Pedro Teixeira, with 2,500 men — soldiers and local people — navigated west along the Amazon River as far as Quito, then under Spanish domination. Along the way he planted several landmarks of occupation on Portugal's behalf. Just over 10 years later, in 1648, another Portuguese colonizer, Raposo Tavares, left southern Brazil heading north for the Solimões River. He arrived in Pará, in northeastern Amazonia, three years later.

Although Spanish and Portuguese adventurers mounted frequent expeditions through Amazonia during the 16th and 17th centuries, it was Catholic missionaries, mainly Jesuit and Franciscan, who had the greatest European presence in the region during those years. The 18th century, however, brought interest in Amazonia from other quarters and from different motivations. During the 1740s the French mathematician Charles-Marie de la Condamine spent several years traipsing through the region and wrote a very influential book about the wonders he encountered — including a sticky tree gum that the natives used to make flexible artifacts. It was in fact latex, and a massive rubber boom would transform the economic life of Amazonia during the latter half of the 19th century.

At the beginning of the 19th century, the brilliant German scientist-explorer Alexander von Humboldt collected over 12,000 plant specimens, most of them new to science, in the course of a four-year expedition through Amazonia. Many other such scientist-explorers followed in Humboldt's footsteps, as the Amazon region took a firm and lasting grip on the world's imagination.

Today, Amazonia is at a historical crossroad after many years in which scientific fascination has competed with reckless exploitation of its natural resources — in particular the rape of the rain forest for its coveted hardwoods. It is well understood how critical the world's largest rain forest is for the health of the planet, but immediate human needs and greeds have to date prevailed over an increasing chorus of protest by a world community horrified by the ecological damage that continues to disfigure this precious habitat.

CHAPTER TWO
The Land

From savannah to tropical rain forest

The Amazon basin is almost synonymous with hot, humid rain forest, but it was not always so. In the course of the past 15,000 years (little more than the blinking of an eye in terms of geological time), the climate has veered between the warm and wet (the Amazonia we have always known) and the more temperate. As recently as 3,000 to 5,000 years ago colder ocean currents from the South Atlantic brought cooler, drier weather to the interior. The evidence for this is provided by traces of pollen of that age found in soil sediments that indicate large areas of savannah grasslands where there is now dense rain forest.

At present there is little variation in temperature in Amazonia, with the exception of its southern and western extremities where the temperature sometimes drops suddenly because of intense cold fronts (called *friagem* in Brazil and *surazo* in Bolivia) coming up from the Antarctic region — in consequence of the infamous El Niño weather system off the coast of Peru. The El Niño effect, which was very severe in 1998, can have a dramatic effect on Amazon wildlife, being particularly disastrous for fish. As the wind cools the surface of lakes and rivers, that cold water drops to the bottom and

Above: The blue-fronted amazon (*Amazonia aestiva*) is one of the many colorful birds for which the Amazon is reknown.

Opposite: An example of Amazonian rain forest in the Mato Grosso area. Being so close to the Equator, the sun's energy is the powerhouse of Amazonia's climate, responsible for the exuberance of life in the forest.

Pages 20–21: Pico da Neblina, a peak of 9,888 feet (3,014 m) on the border between Brazil and Venezuela.
Page 21: One of the many waterfalls for which the town Presidente Figueiredo is well known.

Above: Clouds regularly gather around Pico da Neblina, which translated means "Peak of the Fog."

stirs up rotting vegetation there. This releases methane gas which displaces the oxygen in the water. As a result, vast numbers of fish suffocate.

Generally, however, the temperature in the Amazon basin stays within a relatively narrow band between 68°F (20°C) at night, rising to 90°F (32°C) during the afternoon. To all intents and purposes there are no seasons, as those who live in temperate climates understand the term. The year-round average temperature of Amazonia is 80°F (27°C). That may seem pleasantly balmy, but oppressive humidity of more than 80 percent (often more than 90 percent) can make it feel like a steam bath. Lethargy is a common complaint, especially by those who are not acclimatized.

Abundant rainfall

Rainfall typically varies between 90 inches (230 cm) and 150 inches (380 cm), the highest falls affecting the upper Amazon and the eastern slopes of the Andes, where prolonged dry spells are virtually unknown. This weather pattern is caused by the confluence of air with a high moisture content and hot surface temperatures. Similarly, in the Atlantic region, along the coast of the Brazilian state of Pará, heavy rainfall is a regular afternoon occurrence. This is due to sea breezes that pick up when the land temperature becomes much hotter than the sea temperature.

The high rainfall levels might suggest generally overcast skies and a relentless drizzle, but such is not the case. As a rule there is plenty of sunshine, but on an average of 200 days a year the heavens suddenly open, usually for just an hour or so in the early afternoon. When it rains, it pours.

It is nothing unusual to have an inch (2.5 cm) fall in an hour. Rainy and dry seasons vary from one part of Amazonia to another. In its northern reaches, up into Venezuela, June to October is the rainy season, while in the upper Amazon, to the west, the rainy season comes in the other half of the year, February to April. In the south, around the Bolivian Heights, it is at its wettest between December and February, with a monthly rainfall of 35 inches (90 cm) regularly recorded.

Deforestation and its consequences

Toward the latter end of the 20th century the predicament of the Amazon rain forest came right to the top of the environmental agenda, where it remains. There are many complex, interconnected issues involved, but they all center on the immediate and long-term consequences of large-scale deforestation. There are two agents of deforestation: tree felling for timber and surface fires, either accidental or deliberately started to clear land for agriculture, livestock ranching, to establish road or rail links, or to get at mineral resources. Deforestation was rampant between the end of World War II and 1990, but it was thought that the annual toll had leveled off and even fallen during the 1990s, reflecting mounting concern about the ecological consequences. In 1999, however, an alarming report in the authoritative *Nature* magazine claimed that this was a delusion. According to *Nature*, satellite images were missing huge amounts of deforestation because superficial regrowth of vegetation in forest gaps masked the grim truth on the ground, where logging and burning continued apace and unseen. *Nature* estimated that logging was destroying 4,000–6,000 square miles (10,000–15,000 sq km) of rain forest a year, with surface fires taking an equivalent toll. This was about double previous estimates, and equates to an area twice the size of Connecticut.

This relentless assault on the Amazonian rain forest has a number of serious consequences, some of them immediate. It destroys precious flora and fauna in a region that is home to the greatest diversity of plants, birds and insects in the world — an untold number of them unknown to science. It also encroaches on indigenous peoples who have managed to live fruitfully for thousands of years well away from the roar of modern life.

Quite apart from the immediate loss of habitat caused by deforestation on such a scale, experts point to catastrophes already on the horizon and just over it. Large tracts of denuded rain forest do not regenerate themselves as rain forests but are "reincarnated" as scrubby savannah. Except in pockets, the soil is not suitable for sustained agriculture and after a few seasons is abandoned.

Where once it was filtered through rain forest canopy, direct sunlight now bakes the ground and raises the air temperature. Because an estimated half of Amazonia's rainfall is a direct result of the evaporation cycle of the forest, precipitation is sharply reduced.

Living rain forest soaks up vast quantities of carbon dioxide, which is the main greenhouse gas. Burning and smoldering rain forest, on the other hand, pours carbon

Above: The forest of the *terra firme* in Araguaia National Park, on Bananal, a huge island in the middle of the Amazon River.

Above, left and opposite: Deforestation through fire and logging destroys vast tracts of the Amazon rain forest every year. Often it is the building of roads for industry, or to encourage settlement, that opens up new areas of the forest and leads to more rapid destruction.

dioxide right back into the atmosphere. This exacerbates the greenhouse effect, which further ratchets up the temperature. This is a vicious circle and climatologists predict that widespread desertification and drought will surely follow, citing in evidence the northeastern coastal region. There deforestation is almost complete, with at most 5 percent of the original rain forest intact. The exhausted land is largely incapable of providing a living, which has forced the inhabitants to abandon the area. At a global level, the greenhouse effect is the principal cause of global warming, which unchecked threatens to melt the polar ice caps with luridly imaginable consequences for the planet.

Above left and right: Many environmental problems are a consequence of deforestation and forest fires; among them is the increased air temperature in the Amazonian region. Studies indicate that those temperatures have already increased by 2.34°F (just over 1°C) and there has been a decrease in the amount of rainfall, with disastrous consequences for the plants and animals that live there.

Opposite: Indigenous settlements have been threatened by wildcat miners demanding access to rich mineral deposits beneath the soil.

Riches under the soil

El Dorado may be a myth, but the geological history of Amazonia created an extraordinary wealth of mineral resources that have only in recent decades been seriously exploited, and whose full potential remains unquantifiable. There are the largest iron ore deposits in the world, as well as huge reserves of cassiterite (tin), manganese, bauxite (aluminum) and copper. It has been estimated that up to two million gold prospectors scour the region for the precious metal. Currently, Brazil is the world's fourth largest producer of gold. In Amazonia as a whole, mining generates more income than any other form of economic activity. The huge Carajas Mining Project southwest of Belém covers a vast area of rain forest in the eastern Amazon and produces around 35 million tons of iron ore a year. A network of road and rail then transports the iron ore to the coast.

In the west of Amazonia there are gold and tin deposits in Rondônia; gold, tin and diamonds in Roraima, zirconium in Amazonas; and niobium and gold along the upper Rio Negro. In 2000, Brazil's total mineral output generated $9.3 billion, making

Above: A mountain of iron ore awaits loading on the railroad that will take it from deep in the rain forest to the coast for shipping around the world.

Opposite: This huge open-cast mine is just one small part of the vast complex of mining activities that make up the Carajas project.

up 1.6 percent of the country's gross domestic product. The sector employs 940,000 workers, excluding the estimated 700,000 *garimpeiros* thought to be active. While mineral resources are nonrenewable, they are very valuable and therefore essential to the economic prosperity of countries that possess them. There is no doubt that large-scale mining activities, under well-regulated conditions, have an important part to play in the sustainable development of Amazonia.

Mining activities have played their part in the depredations suffered by the rain forest, however. In particular, gold strikes in central Brazil in the 1980s brought a swarm of wildcat miners (*garimpeiros*) inflamed with gold rush fever. Like a plague of locusts they stripped everything bare, destroying rivers and forests alike with jet-nozzle pumps and diesel-powered dredges. Some of these miners also forced indigenous peoples off their land and killed those that stood in their way. Even worse, by illegally using mercury in their makeshift gold-purifying process they left a deadly legacy of mercury poisoning in the food chain.

Amazonian lands also possesses an abundance of energy resources in the form of hydrocarbons (oil and natural gas). In the 1970s, prospecting along the Rio Juruá established the existence of considerable reserves of these coveted resources. Amazonas state also holds rich deposits along the Urucu River. It is estimated that these two areas alone make up 50 percent of Brazil's total natural gas reserves. There are proven oil and gas reserves in the western Amazon basin, along the Ecuador–Colombia frontier and in Bolivia. As with mining, it is economically essential to exploit such known resources, although ecological considerations come to bear on the construction of pipelines. At the beginning of the 21st century, Brazil began selling off oil exploration rights to foreign companies, ending a period of 45 years during which oil was the jealous preserve of a state-owned monopoly.

Pages 32–33: Gold mining in the middle of the forest. Gold is an important source of income for the countries that make up Amazonia. When gold was discovered along the Brazilian–Venezuelan border in the 1970s it sparked the single biggest gold rush in history. This gold rush continues today, and the expansion of mining operations into previously pristine rain forest has brought the governments involved considerable criticism from environmentalists worldwide. The situation made international headlines when the plight of the Yanomami people, who were being forced from their lands and sometimes killed, became a focus for protest.

CHAPTER THREE
The Rivers

The mightiest river in the world

The Amazon springs to life among myriad streams high in the Peruvian Andes, some of them within 100 miles (160 km) of the Pacific Ocean. From their starting point at an altitude of over 17,000 feet (5,150 m) these streams rush down the eastern slopes of the mountains, continually merging to form ever-larger torrents and eventually a majestic river of awesome proportions. By the time the waters reach their destination in the Atlantic Ocean they have meandered the width of the continent and a distance of over 4,000 miles (6,400 km). Exactly how far is a matter of dispute since the answer hangs upon the Amazon's claim to be the longest river in the world. Geography books have traditionally given the honor to the Nile, claiming that at 4,160 miles (6,697 km) it is nearly a hundred miles (160 km) the longer of the two. However the Amazon has a number of mouths, and if the measurement is taken at the Pará estuary it lengthens the Amazon to 4,195 miles (6,750 km).

Making no allowance for national bias, it seems reasonable to accept the Amazon as the longest river since it is incomparably the greatest by any other measurement. It is fed by water from more than 1,000 named tributaries (and many times as many anonymous ones) that include 12 rivers of more than 1,000 miles (1,600 km) in length. It drains around 60 percent of Brazil and more than half of Bolivia and Peru, along with

Above: Mariuá is the largest riverine archipelago in the world, with 1,266 islands distributed along 87 miles (140 km) of the Rio Negro.

Opposite: Along some stretches of the Amazon the distance between banks reaches over 31 miles (50 km).

Pages 34–35: View of the Cristalino River, Alta Floresta, in the province of Mato Grosso.
Page 35: Blue-and-yellow macaw (*Ara ararauna*).

Above: A member of the Jaru community, Rio Negro. The impenetrable rain forest means that the rivers and river channels are the "roads" of Amazonia, providing access to even the most remote areas.

Opposite: The rivers of Amazonia teem with life. One of the most distinctive of its animals is the *peixe boi* or manatee.

much of Ecuador, Colombia and Venezuela and portions of Guyana, Suriname and French Guiana. This is a total area of just over 2,722,000 square miles (7 million sq km), which is nearly the size of Australia. It discharges into the Atlantic approximately one-fifth of the total continental runoff of all rivers on the planet (some 12 times the discharge of the Mississippi). So massive is the discharge that it measurably dilutes the salinity of the ocean for more than 100 miles (160 km) out to sea. Suspended sediments ejected from the mouth of the Amazon have been found near the Florida coast, and traces of dissolved nutrients from it are carried as far north as the Grand Banks of Newfoundland.

The list of superlatives stretches on. It is navigable from Iquitos in eastern Peru to the mouth at Belém, a distance of 2,300 miles (3,700 km), the longest stretch of navigable inland waterway in the world. There are 50,000 miles (80,000 km) of navigable rivers in the Amazon system. The average width is about 3 miles (5 km) but downstream in Brazil it can reach 40 miles (65 km) in the mainstream. The Amazon's depth varies greatly with seasonal flooding, but the mainstream remains deep enough for very deep-draft ocean-going ships to reach Manaus in central Brazil, 1,000 miles (1,600 km) upstream throughout the year. Shallow-draft freighters and passenger ships drawing less than 14 feet (4.25 m) can go all the way to Iquitos. The Amazon's deepest point, 300 feet (90 m), is near Manaus where the Rio Negro meets the mainstream.

Moving downstream from Iquitos, the Amazon begins its winding, sluggish progress across lowland plains. The reason for the sluggishness is that in the great distance from Iquitos to the coast it drops only 230 feet (70 m). The gradient is so shallow that the river scarcely flows at all as a consequence of gravity, but gets its push from the annual rush of thawed snow pouring down from the Andes. From Iquitos to Manaus the river is known locally as the Solimões, and only from Manaus to the Atlantic as the Amazon. The Solimões is augmented by the Japurá coming in from the north and the Juruá and Purus joining from the south. Manaus, the principal crossroads of Amazonia, is at the confluence of the Solimões and the mighty Rio Negro, one of the world's great rivers in its own right.

The Negro gets its name from the color of its water, which is very dark, stained with dissolved organic matter, but sediment-free so very clear. In contrast the silt-laden Solimões, called a "white" river to distinguish it and its tributaries from the "black" rivers of the Negro system, is in fact a murky yellow or brown. Where the "black" and "white" waters join up at Manaus this "meeting of the waters" provides a wondrous

sight. For several miles downstream the two distinctively colored waters flow side by side before slowly merging into the uniform pale brown of the Amazon. A steady succession of tributaries entering from both sides — most notably the majestic Madeira, yet another of the world's greatest rivers — continue to swell the flow as the Amazon continues its unhurried progress to the Atlantic.

Because it is ultimately controlled by melting snow in the Andes, river levels rise and fall according to the seasons. They begin to rise in November, peaking in April–May. Then they slowly subside, reaching their lowest levels in October, before starting to rise again. At Iquitos the difference between low and high watermarks can be as much as 30 feet (9 m). At Manaus it can be more; in 1989 it was measured at 45 feet (13.5 m).

As it nears the mouth the Amazon splits up into countless shifting, silt-laden channels clogged with islands large and small. The largest of these delta islands, Marajó, covers 19,500 square miles (50,000 sq km), which is more than twice the size of Vermont. The main channel, to the north of Marajó, is the scene of a great bore or tidal wave, the *pororoca*. As the incoming ocean tide rolls over top of the outgoing river, huge waves up to 18 feet (5.5 m) form, and the violent upheaval can be heard for miles. The name is taken from the local people and means "big roar." The *pororoca* is at its most dramatic around the March equinox and very high tides can send the waves rushing hundreds of miles inland, making it the most powerful tidal bore in the world.

The Sweet Sea

The first European sighting of the Amazon was in 1500. The experienced Spanish navigator Vicente Pinzón, who had sailed with Columbus on the epic voyage of 1492, was returning to the Spanish discoveries in the Caribbean when he strayed off course to the south. At a certain point Pinzón noticed that the seawater was almost fresh, so he turned west toward the distant, low-lying coast. This brought him to the mouth of the Amazon, and he is thought to have sailed up it perhaps 50 miles (80 km) before turning back for the Atlantic and his destination to the north. Pinzón did, however, leave for posterity a poetic description of the great river: he named it the Sweet Sea.

Above: The spectacular meeting of the "black" waters of the Rio Negro and the "white" Solimões River.

Opposite: The dramatic *pororoca*, brought about by the clash between the current of the river and the sea's incoming tide.

CHAPTER FOUR
The Forest

Above: Nearly 2,500 different species of trees have been observed in the Amazonian forest, which also shelters over 300 species of mammals. Around 2,000 kinds of fish live in the rivers of the region, and 2,000 species of birds fly over this paradise of life.

The great repository of life

The Amazonian rain forest contains the greatest diversity of life forms in the world — and the diversity runs right across the biological spectrum. It is home to more than 300 mammal species and up to 2,000 kinds of birds (that is about double the number of bird species in North America and Europe combined). There are an estimated 2,000 species of fish in its waters, many of them still not cataloged. The number of insect species is incalculable, but some estimates go as high as 30 million (the overwhelming majority as yet unclassified). So much for the animal kingdom. The plant kingdom is equally well represented in the rain forest. There are some 2,500 species of trees along with perhaps 60,000 distinct plants (again whole swathes of them unclassified).

The three main types of Amazon rain forest are the *várzea*, the *igapó* and the *terra firme*. The two former are both floodplain zones — regions that are regularly submerged. The *várzea*, which is flooded by the nutrient-rich white rivers, has much greater species differentiation than the *igapó*, which is flooded by the largely sediment-free black rivers. The floodplain zones are especially important for the fish of the region and the fishing industry in general. Although principally harvested in the main river channels or far downstream in the estuaries, many commercial species spawn only on the floodplain; predatory fish rely on prey that migrate seasonally from the floodplain to

Opposite: Often the easiest and best way to see the rain forest is from one of the thousands of river channels.

Pages 42–43: All along the rivers of the Amazon people build their houses to take advantage of the bounty of the forest and the river.

Page 43: *Sumaúma* (*Ceiba pentandra*), one of the giants of the rain forest.

Above: Brilliantly colored beetles abound in the rain forest, where thousands of insect species await discovery and classification.

Opposite: Amphibians and reptiles, such the *jacarés açu*, or black caiman inhabit the low layers of the flooded Amazonian forest (right).

the river channels; and many fish gorge themselves on the fruits and seeds that fall during the floods.

Terra firme, which forms about 90 percent of the rain forest, is not flooded in the rainy season, and it is there that the greatest number of species are found. For example the *terra firme* of northwestern Amazonia is believed to have the greatest diversity of tree species in the world (acre for acre, about 10 times the number found in a temperate forest).

This is the classic rain forest of the imagination, where teeming plant and animal life coexist in a series of horizontal layers from the canopy down to the floor. While giant mahogany, teak and others thrust themselves high above the rest, when it is seen from the air the canopy appears a nearly uniform sea of green, the slender canopy trees standing almost shoulder to shoulder, so narrow are their crowns, and never overlapping neighbors of the same species. Beneath the canopy is a shrub layer, in virgin forest only sparsely populated by saplings, shrubs, small palms and tree ferns. Where the forest has been felled, scrubby regrowth is much denser. At ground level, which in virgin forest is almost completely cut off from sunlight and comprises only a thin layer of nutrient-poor soil, ferns, herbs and seedlings are the only plants to survive, along with fungi.

From the ground up live nonclimbers and climbers, such as tapirs and tortoises, armadillos and tree sloths, snakes and the elusive jaguar. Above them the canopy is alive with the cries of monkeys and a breathtaking variety of bird life, including tiny whizzing hummingbirds, raucous, brilliantly plumaged parrots and massively beaked toucans.

Symbols of threatened extinction

The noble jaguar and the mighty mahogany tree are perhaps the best-known representatives of Amazonian fauna and flora under threat of extinction or savage depletion. The largest New World feline, a male jaguar can grow to a length of 6 feet (183 cm), excluding the tail which adds 30 inches (76 cm). Compact and very powerfully built, the mature jaguar stands 2 feet (60 cm) at the shoulder and may weigh some 250 pounds (114 kg). This solitary predator stands at the top of the food chain, equally adept at swimming and climbing for its prey. The jaguar loomed large in the pre-Columbian civilizations of South and Central America, where it was worshiped as a god for its

Opposite: Estimates indicate that thousands of species of fauna and flora disappear with the felling of the forest. The *onça pintada*, or jaguar, the largest feline in the Americas, is one of the most endangered species of Amazonia. It can reach over 8 feet (2.5 m) in length, when its tail is included, and weigh up to 250 pounds (114 kg). It has almost disappeared from other Brazilian ecosystems, and just a very few specimens survive in Argentina, Costa Rica and Panama.

Above: A good example of the flooded *igápo* forest can be seen on the Anavilhanas Archipelago, on the Rio Negro, where nearly 400 islands create a breathtaking natural labyrinth.

Opposite: Another symbol of the destruction of Amazonia is the mahogany. A large tree, which can reach a height of 130 feet (40 m), the mahogany is the victim of indiscriminate exploitation due to its high economic worth. Today, the largest concentrations of the species are in Bolivia and Brazil.

power and beauty. Already extinct over much its former range, this majestic, rare creature is under a three-pronged attack in the fastness of its Amazonian habitat. First, deforestation is shrinking the available habitat. Second, ranchers claim that jaguars attack cattle (they do, but infrequently) and shoot them — despite the endangered species status of the jaguar. Third, poachers supplying the demand for exotic furs kill an estimated 6,000 annually. They tend to hunt beneath a cloak of darkness, blinding their victims with powerful searchlights and even using advanced night-imaging equipment.

The fact that there are some 2,500 logging companies and sawmills in the Amazon region indicates the scale of the assault on the great ancient trees of the rain forest — the imposing mahogany foremost amongst them. Mahogany has always been much coveted for the beautiful reddish brown color of its timber, and it commands a high price. While Brazilian exports of the wood began in a small way in the 1920s, it was not until the completion of the Belém-Brasilia Highway in 1960 that deforestation really got under way (although initially the main goal was not to get timber so much as it was to clear the way for settlement and ranching). Typically, entire stands of mahogany were felled at a stroke, leaving none standing to propagate and therefore begin the process of regeneration. Today, there is much greater awareness of the need for the timber industry to adopt sustainable extraction practices, but illegal logging activities are commonplace and it takes many years for a mahogany tree to reach its mature height of 130 feet (40 m) or more.

Until the 1980s almost all tropical wood exported throughout the world came from the rain forests of Southeast Asia, with West African rain forests a distant second. At that time Amazonia scarcely exported tropical wood at all, but used its increasing timber output for domestic purposes. However the 1980s marked a critical period where those other two great rain forests were seen to be shrinking at a perilous rate. Increasingly, the markets for tropical woods turned their eyes on the greatest rain forest of them all. But large-scale logging operations immediately came under fire from the burgeoning environmentalist movement, and Amazonian mahogany became a specific target for concern under the umbrella slogan, "Save the rain forest."

Far right and opposite: Assai palm (*Euterpe olearacea*).
Right: The fruit of the *pupunha* or peach palm (*Bactris gasipaes*).
Below right: *Sumaúma* (*Ceiba pentandra*).

Some illustrious inhabitants of the largest forest in the world

Amazonia embraces the richest ecosystem on the planet, and by far the greatest bio-diversity. In almost every respect its flora and fauna seem to be exceptional. In the following pages you will see the largest flower in the world, the most enormous snake, the biggest rodent and the largest of all parrots.

Assai palm, açai palm   EUTERPE OLEARACEA

This is an imposing palm tree that reaches over 80 feet (24 m) in height. It is a most versatile tree in terms of the uses to which it is put. The heart of the tree (*palmito*) is edible. The roots are used as a vermicide (it kills worms). The seeds make excellent fertilizers, while the tough leaves are used by *caboclos* (backwoodsmen) to thatch their houses. The fruit is highly nutritious and is used to prepare delicious desserts and drinks, including açai wine.

Pupunha, peach palm   BACTRIS GASIPAES

This palm tree can grow to a height of 60 feet (18 m) and its wood is used by Amazonians in the construction of their homes. The leaves are used as a condiment, while the fruit, eaten cooked, is prized as a food rich in vitamin A.

Sumaúma   CEIBA PENTANDRA

This majestic tree is one of the true giants of Amazonia, soaring to a height of 130 feet (40 m) and with a diameter of up to 6 feet (180 cm). Its wood is light and white, and is used to make boxes, buoys and toys. An edible oil is extracted from its seeds.

Far left: Guaraná (*Paullinia cupana*).
Left: Amazon water lily (*Victoria amazonica*).
Below left: Cacao tree (*Theobroma cacao*).

Amazon water lily, Victoria water lily

VICTORIA AMAZONICA

The giant water lily is a great symbol of Amazonia, where it is the queen of the swamp-lands. The lily pad can grow to a diameter of 6½ feet (2 m) while the flower itself, at nearly a foot (30 cm) in diameter, is the largest in the world. When it opens it is white and powerfully scented, but as soon as it is pollinated it darkens to a deep mauve/purple and loses its scent.

Guaraná

PAULLINIA CUPANA

This is a kind of creeper that covers the trees in the forest, and it can also be found on the ground in shrub form in adjacent savannah regions. Its famous red seeds are used to make a nutritious powder, which is a popular ingredient in energy drinks around the world.

Cacao tree

THEOBROMA CACAO

The powdered fruit seeds of this tree are the basis for satisfying one the world's most powerful cravings — for chocolate. The seeds, commonly called cocoa beans, are inside pods that can grow to 10 inches (25 cm) long and weigh two pounds (nearly 1 kg) or so. Cocoa is high in food value and is mildly stimulating (as well as delicious) because it contains an alkaloid closely related to caffeine.

Orchids

There are more than 2,500 species of these highly prized plants in Amazonia, with the greatest diversity in the upland forest regions that are sometimes called "cloud forest." Famed for their gorgeous blooms, orchids are usually difficult to spot from the ground because they tend to grow on tree branches high up in the canopy.

Urucu
BIXA ORELLANA

For thousands of years indigenous Amazonians have used the intense red dye obtainable from the seeds of this shrub to decorate their bodies. They also mix the pulp surrounding the seeds with fish oil and smear it on their skin as an insect repellent. Urucu contains an effective UVR filter as well, which is of commercial value for use in sunscreens and cosmetic products.

Rubber tree
HEVEA BRASILIENSIS

The milky-white latex from this famous tree is the raw material for the production of rubber. The tree is native to the Amazon, and when the rubber-making process was perfected in the 19th century it triggered a massive economic boom in the hitherto neglected heart of Amazonia.

Boto, Amazon river dolphin, pink dolphin INIA GEOFFRENSIS

The larger of the two freshwater dolphins that inhabit the Amazon, the pink dolphin can reach 8 feet (2.5 m) and weigh 350 pounds (160 kg). It likes to cruise slowly along the bottom, using its unique sonar sensory equipment to search for fish and crustacea. The bulging forehead is a sonar weapon as well as a detector, bombarding and stunning prey with high-frequency sound bursts. Fearsome predators like their saltwater cousins, they are generally less playful with humans.

The gray dolphin (*Sotalia fluviatilis*) is the smaller of the two river dolphins. It reaches a length of 5 feet (1.5 m) and weighs about 110 pounds (50 kg). In contrast to the bottom-feeding pink dolphin it displays the agility associated with dolphins generally, and is adept at catching quick-moving fish near the surface.

Giant catfish or piraibi BRACHYPLATHYSTOMA FILAMENTOSUM

This is the largest of the thousand or so species of catfish found in the Amazon and its tributaries. While the tiniest of these catfish are less than $^1/_4$ inch (6 mm) in length, the huge piraibi, as it is known locally, can reach a length of 10 feet (3 m) and weigh more than 350 pounds (160 kg). It is highly prized by anglers because of its tremendous fighting qualities, as well as being important to commercial fishing.

Amazonian manatee TRICHECHUS INUNGUIS

The gentle giant of the Amazon, this ponderous herbivore can reach a length of 10 feet (3 m) and tip the scales at over half a ton (500 kg). As it swims slowly along just beneath the surface with its nostrils breaking the water to breathe, the manatee makes easy prey for *caboclos* who harpoon them from boats, usually at night. Immensely strong, the injured manatee drags its assailant along until exhaustion sets in. The hunter then stuffs wooden plugs into his victim's nostrils, causing suffocation. While manatee are an endangered species they are still exploited as a cash food crop.

Top: Boto (*Inia geoffrensis*).

Above: Giant catfish (*Brachyplathystoma filamentosum*).

Opposite: Manatee (*Trichechus inunguis*).

Tambaqui
COLOSSOMA MACROPOMUM

This is a favorite of Amazonian cuisine, and makes up some 40 percent of the fish consumed in the Manaus region, where it thrives on seeds and small fruits which it can crush with its small teeth. It is a large fish, up to 3 feet (90 cm) in length and weighing 65 pounds (30 kg).

Piranha
SERRASALMUS SPP.

There are two dozen species of piranha, most of them innocuous vegetarians, but it is the voracious red-bellied piranha (*Serrasalmus nattereri*) that has invaded the nightmares of the outside world. They may be small, about 8 inches (20 cm) in length, but they come awesomely equipped with a mouthful of sharp, serrated teeth (natives use them as cutting tools). Piranhas have to keep those teeth honed by frequent use, otherwise they grow too large. The piranha's lurid reputation is overdrawn, and Amazonians coexist in the water with them, if warily. Nevertheless, when they are in concentrated numbers and taste blood the ensuring feeding frenzy can be astonishing in its intensity. A large animal carcass can be stripped in minutes.

Black caiman, jacaré açu
MELANOSUCHUS NIGER

The largest New World caiman has a length of up to 16 feet (5 m) and is in danger of extinction. It feeds on fish, birds, mammals and other reptiles and has a voracious taste for piranhas.

Top: Tambaqui (*Colossoma macropomum*).
Above: Piranha (*Serrasalmus* spp.).
Opposite: Black caiman (*Melanosichus niger*).

Coral snake
ELAPIDAE

Its bold red, white and black bands gives ample visual warning of the presence of this beautiful but venomous snake. There are some 50 species of coral snake, and they are members of the cobra family. They do not exceed 4 feet (1.2 m) in length, and their bite, while painful, is rarely life-threatening to healthy humans.

Anaconda, sucuri
EUNECTES MURINUS

This nonvenomous constrictor is the world's largest snake, reaching a maximum length of about 33 feet (10 m) and weighing a colossal 500 pounds (about 225 kg). Because of its extraordinary size, the anaconda has always been portrayed as a sort of prehistoric monster — tall tales abound in Amazonia (and Hollywood) about giant anacondas dropping out of trees and encircling hapless victims in a deadly embrace, or devouring shipwrecked crews in their entirety.

Boa constrictor
CONSTRICTOR CONSTRICTOR

As its name implies, this large snake squeezes the life out of its prey before swallowing it whole. Even with a length of up to 13 feet (4 m) boas are not really big enough to tackle humans unless desperate, so well-fed specimens are often welcome around the house since they keep down the rodent population.

Top left: Red-legged tortoise (*Geochelone carbonaria*).

Top right: Giant otter (*Pteronura brasiliensis*).

Above: Common zorro (*Cerdocyon thous*).

Opposite top left: A young tapir (*Tapirus terrestris*).

Opposite top right: Capybara family group
(*Hydrochoerus hydrochaeris*).

Opposite bottom right: Three-toed sloth with young
(*Bradypus tridactylus*).

Red-legged tortoise   GEOCHELONE CARBONARIA

This tortoise and the closely related yellow-legged tortoise (*G. denticulata*) are endemic to the Amazon region. Their preferred habitat is shaded forest, and these tortoises can be found in damp, muddy dens. The shell of the red-legged tortoise is around 20 inches (50 cm). Both species have almost been driven to extinction by indiscriminate hunting for their meat, and efforts are being made to save them through a captive breeding program.

Common zorro, crab-eating fox   CERDOCYON THOUS

At around 3 feet (1 m) in length, including tail, and 14 to 16 pounds (6 to 7 kg), this small member of the dog family was once a familiar sight in Amazonia. Today, how-ever, this skillful predator is very rarely seen. They live and hunt in packs and are mainly nocturnal, feeding on small rodents, lizards, frogs, crabs, eggs and fruit.

Giant otter   PTERONURA BRASILIENSIS

The world's largest otter can weigh as much as 75 pounds (34 kg). It has a voracious appetite for fish, and the swimming ability and sharp teeth to satisfy it. Partly for this reason, and also because there is a ready market for otter pelts, these playful, friendly animals have been persecuted to the brink of extinction.

Tapir
TAPIRUS TERRESTRIS

The tapir, a distant relative of the horse, is the largest indigenous animal in the rain forest, standing a little over 3 feet (1 m) at the shoulder and weighing as much as 550 pounds (250 kg). Heavy-bodied and short-legged, tapirs are keenly hunted for their meat so tend to stay out of sight, making a rush for nearby water if disturbed.

Capybara
HYDROCHOERUS HYDROCHAERIS

The largest rodent in the world can tip the scales at up to 250 pounds (113 kg). It looks like an oversize guinea pig, and in fact makes a docile pet for Amazonians. It feeds on riverside vegetation, and is an excellent swimmer. The capybara is plentiful as well as edible, and bred commercially could form part of a sustainable rain forest economy.

Three-toed sloth
BRADYPUS TRIDACTYLUS

Sloths, of which there are four species in Amazonia, are primitive mammals related to anteaters. They are very slow moving (slothful in fact), and spend almost all of their time hanging by their powerful limbs from branches of cecropia trees, whose leaves are its favorite food. Sloths are good swimmers but are very vulnerable to predators on the ground, where they have to drag themselves around slowly using their claws.

Above left: Pygmy marmoset (*Callithrix pygmaea*).

Above right: Spider monkey (*Ateles paniscus*).

Pygmy marmoset
CALLITHRIX PYGMAEA

Sometimes called the world's smallest monkey, this is in fact the smallest of the marmosets, which are close relatives but not true monkeys. They really are tiny, about 6 inches (15 cm) from top to toe and weighing maybe 4 ounces (110 g). Locally the pygmy marmoset is nicknamed *leoncito* (little lion) because of its reddish yellow mane. These cute little animals are very popular pets in Amazonia.

Spider monkey, macaco aranha
ATELES PANISCUS

Spider monkeys have an exceptionally long tail and legs relative to their body, with a prehensile and extremely flexible tail. They live high in the forest canopy, and only the gibbon exceeds this monkey in agility. Their diet is mainly fruit, supplemented with nuts, seeds, flowers and insects.

Sauim-de-coleira
SAGUINUS BICOLOR

In danger of extinction, this tiny monkey can only be found in the vicinity of Manaus, the captial of Amazonas. It lives within a family group and the female has around two offspring a year. They feed mainly on nectar, small fruits and insects.

Capuchin monkey, macaco prego CEBUS APELLA

Capuchins are known for their intelligence and ability to learn quickly. Small, stockily built monkeys, they are 12 to 22 inches (30 to 55 cm) long, with a tail of about the same length. They are very active in the high canopy of the rain forest, living in groups of up to 30 individuals. Fruit, leaves, bark and insects form the main part of their diet.

Woolly monkey, macaco barrigudo LAGOTHRIX LAGOTRICHA

This monkey is one of the largest American primates, weighing up to 24 pounds (10 kg), and has a covering of short, thick fur that varies in color from dark gray, through brown to sandy yellow. Preferring mature undisturbed rain forest, they are under threat from increasing encroachment by development, as well as the trade in exotic pets.

Above left: Sauim-de-coleira (*Saguinus bicolor*).

Above right: Capuchin monkey (*Cebus apella*).

Squirrel monkey, macaco-de-cheiro SAIMIRI SCIUREUS

This tiny monkey is barely 15 inches (6 cm) tall and weighs just over 2 pounds (1 kg). It is very popular as a pet with children and can be seen in most villages in Amazonia. In the wild, they live in large groups, of up to 45 individuals, and inhabit the margins where the forest and savannah meet.

White uakari CACAJAO CALVUS CALVUS

This rare monkey and its cousin the red uakari are the only monkeys in the Americas without a long tail. With its bright red, wrinkled face it looks a little like a sad clown. Its habitat is restricted to the islands of the upper Amazon, where it is endangered.

Above left: Squirrel monkey (*Saimiri sciureus*).
Above right: White uakari (*Cacajao calvus calvus*).
Opposite: Woolly monkey (*Lagothrix lagotricha*).

Scarlet macaw

ARA MACAO

Macaws are the largest members of the parrot family, and the brilliant-hued scarlet macaw is the picture-postcard Amazonian parrot. It is widely distributed through the Amazon basin, where it nests in the hollow trunks of palm trees, whose fruit provides its food. At risk through habitat destruction, poaching for food and feathers and the illegal trading of live birds, the scarlet macaw is part of international efforts to ensure its survival.

Blue-and-gold macaw

ARA ARARAUNA

This species is the largest of the macaws, reaching a length of $3^3/4$ feet (1.2 m). Like the scarlet macaw it makes its home in hollow trees. Their natural habitat ranges from Panama in Central America south to Bolivia, Brazil and Paraguay. As with all macaws, they are noisy birds and are part of the clamor of the rain forest at dawn and dusk.

Blue-fronted amazon, turquoise-fronted parrot, papagayo   AMAZONIA AESTIVA

Each year thousands of blue-fronted amazon chicks are taken for the illegal trade in exotic birds, and efforts are being made to monitor this problem and recover birds for return to the wild. This beautiful parrot is about 14 inches (35 cm) long, with a green body, yellow patches at the top of the wings and a patch of blue just above the beak.

Top left: Scarlet macaw (*Ara macao*).

Bottom left: Blue-and-gold macaw (*Ara ararauna*).

Opposite: Blue-fronted amazon (*Amazonia aestiva*).

Channel-billed toucan
RAMPHASTOS VITELLINUS

These fabulous-looking birds stand out even in the crowd of exotic Amazonian bird life. Their bills can be as long as their bodies (the largest in relation to their size of any bird). That gigantic bill is, however, very light since it is largely hollow, with a honeycombed structure to give it strength. While toucans are omnivorous, they mainly use those mighty bills to pluck berries and other fruit from the ends of branches.

Cock-of-the-rock
RUPICOLA SPP.

This beautiful bird is a skilled dancer. The male displays to the female with a series of quick runs and small leaps, at the climax of which he opens his beautiful fan, just as a peacock would do. It is said that its striking gold plumage used to decorate the cloaks of royalty.

Uirapuru
CYPHORHINUS ARADUS

This little songbird has a voice so melodious that the other birds in the forest are said to stop singing just to listen to it. Its charm has inspired several legends among

Amazonians, one in particular that is greatly to the bird's disadvantage. A lotion made from the charred remains of its body is said to be a powerful talisman, capable of melting an indifferent heart. Consequently these birds often meet an untimely end.

King vulture, urubu rei   SARCORAMPHUS PAPA

This dramatic-looking bird is the largest of the American vultures, excluding the condor, with a wingspan of 4 to 5 feet (1.2 to 1.5 m). Their preferred habitat is dense lowland rain forest, and these birds can spend hours riding the thermals over the forest searching for carrion. As development impacts on their habitat, the future of the king vulture is in peril.

Harpy eagle, gavião real   HARPIA HARPYJA

This the largest eagle and most powerful bird of prey in the world. It is just under 3 feet (1 m) long and has a wingspan of over 6 feet (2 m). Their claws are the size of a human hand, with talons 5 inches (12.5 cm) long — making them a fearsome predator of the rain forest. Their main prey are sloths, monkeys, large reptiles and other birds.

Insects are well represented among the wealth of the Amazonian fauna: from beetles to stick insects, weevils and grasshoppers, to wasps, butterflies and caterpillars. Many thousands of species have not yet been named.

74

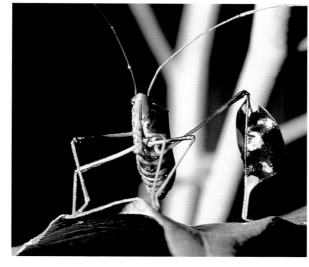

CHAPTER FIVE

The People

A fascinating mixture of peoples

It is a common misconception that Amazonia is largely uninhabited, and always has been. In fact, at the beginning of the 21st century some 30 million people inhabited the Amazon basin. So while that is scarcely tooth-by-jowl living, it is a far cry from being unpopulated. By way of comparison Australia, which covers a similar area, has a population of about 20 million.

A little over half of the Amazonian population is urban, largely distributed among the old established centers that date back to colonial times or, more recently, the 19th-century rubber boom. Manaus, the capital of the Brazilian state of Amazonas and the largest and most important city in the whole region, has a population of more than 1.5 million. Belém, the gateway to the Amazon, is only a little smaller and Iquitos, the world's most inland port, is a bustling center too.

Perhaps one-fifth of Amazonia's population is made up of small farmers (*campesinos*). This is a shifting population, much of it migratory in pursuit of seasonal work, almost all of it poor, reflecting the agricultural realities of the Amazon basin — thin soil lacking in nutrients and easily exhausted by conventional crop-growing. In the 1960s and 1970s it was naively thought that *campesinos* and large ranchers between them could "tame" the rain forest and make it productive, in the sense that farmland

Pages 76–79: Amazonia has been inhabited for at least 11,500 years. During the times of the European invasions, the region was the home of about five million people, distributed in 1,400 groups that spoke 1,300 different dialects. At present, only 180 ethnic groups remain, divided into six linguistic branches. These photographs show peoples living within the Xingu Indigenous Park in southeastern Brazil.

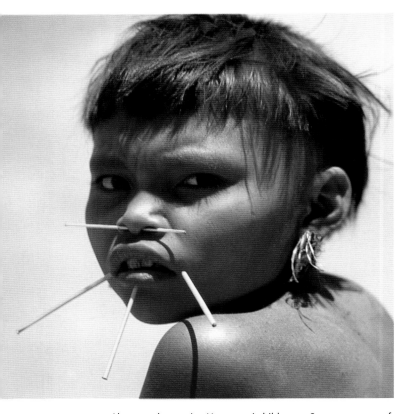

Above and opposite: Yanomami children at Surucucus, part of the Yanomami homelands in northern Amazonia. Frequent and violent incursions into Yanomami territory by gold miners since the 1980s put their future under threat.

was considered productive (as opposed to "unproductive" forest). Today the ruinous consequences of such a policy are easy to see in the denuded forests and deserted farms of the coastal region. *Campesinos* can be seen traipsing from one rural colonization project to another, then moving on as that too fails, often winding up living hand-to-mouth in urban centers. Faced with such a cycle of dreary disappointment it is little wonder that some *campesinos* turn their hands to the production of coca, and so fuel the illegal cocaine traffic.

As a legacy of the gold rush of the 1980s it is estimated that there are anywhere up to two million gold prospectors combing the rivers and streams of the Amazon basin. These *garimpeiros* live a precarious existence, but there are sufficient pickings to generate a gold-based economy where many times their actual number are indirectly involved in the enterprise — from the buying and selling of gold to provisioning to prostitution. As a counterpoint to all this small-scale economic activity there are the large-scale activities of road-building, dam-constructing, mining and logging.

The first Amazonians

Taken together, the modern economic life of the region impinges massively on the indigenous peoples of the Amazon, who number fewer than 700,000, something under half of them in the Brazilian portion of Amazonia. These are the remnants of the earliest Americans who filtered down from the Andes into the lowlands perhaps 12,000 years ago. The archaeological record of Amazonia is very hit-and-miss because the climate is the worst possible for preserving organic remains, as it is for archaeological fieldwork. But pottery remains suggest that almost certainly by 7,000 to 8,000 years ago there was a substantial Amerindian presence along the river ways of Amazonia.

Around this time the four key language groups of the region became dispersed: the Tupi moving north from central Brazil and fanning out across the region to the south of the Amazon; the Ge, displaced by the fierce Tupi, heading west into the upper Amazon; the Carib infiltrating the lower Amazon — either moving down the South American coast from their established home in the Caribbean to the mouth of the river, or taking the longer route across northern South America and then down through the Andes and along the waterways. The Arawak spread down from Central America to occupy the lands southwest of the Rio Negro. There are two more isolated language groups, the Pano who inhabit the western margins of the Amazon rain forest and the Xiriana, which is the language group of the celebrated Yanomami who are confined to an area that straddles the Venezuela–Brazil border.

Estimates of the number of Amerindians inhabiting Amazonia on the eve of the European arrival in 1500 vary wildly, from less than two million to over eight million, in up to 2,000 tribes. They were most densely settled in the floodplain along the main river systems, where they cultivated quick-growing crops of manioc (the ubiquitous root vegetable of Amazonia, which is pounded into a coarse flour) and corn. Fish, too, were plentiful during the dry season, and, preserved in oil, helped tide them over the rainy season.

Over time many natives became assimilated into Amazonia's racial melting pot — most present-day inhabitants have native blood as well as African and European. But those who have retained their tribal identity continue to live much as their forebears did. They are agriculturalists, either in *terra firme* regions of the rain forest or in floodplain.

Those whose habitat is *terra firme* clear small areas of forest with axe and machete and plant manioc, sweet potatoes, plantain and bananas, according to custom and preference. When the soil loses its fertility, as it does after a few seasons, they move on and repeat the process. However, since their crops have different growing times they may return to harvest a long-growing crop. Because the abandoned plots are relatively small, they are in time reclaimed by the rain forest, which means this so-called slash-and-burn type of agriculture, on the scale it is practiced, is a perfectly sustainable use of the rain forest. Agricultural produce is supplemented by hunting and fishing, both of which the Amazonians are very skilled at. Some hunt with bows and arrows, others use spears or blowguns with poisoned darts. Fish are commonly netted, although spears and bows and arrows are sometimes used, as is poisoning.

In floodplain regions, rice, beans and cocoa are staples, along with a quick-growing variety of manioc. The seasonal floods revitalize the soil, while the adjacent rivers provide plentiful fish, turtles and birds, along with mammals who visit the water's edge. Consequently, floodplain

Above and opposite: In the view of the Yanomami, and other native Amazonians, beauty and adornment are part of the harmony of the natural world. Everything in this world exists to "shine brightly," and humans exist to dance and celebrate this shining, which is the essence of the cosmos.

dwellers are not compelled to move from site to site in the way *terra ferme* dwellers are.

While most natives live this sort of settled or at least semi-settled existence, sometimes in communities numbering several hundred, others are more nomadic, relying mainly or entirely on what they can hunt and gather in the forest and harvest from the rivers. Whatever their mode of living, almost all Amazonian tribes have had contact with the outside world, to a greater or lesser extent. But some small groups in the remotest regions of the rain forest — an unknown number, by definition — have managed to avoid all such contact.

The great nation of the Yanomami

To the outside world the Yanomami tribe is perhaps the best known of all the indigenous peoples of Amazonia. The reason is that these seminomadic people, who dwell in a remote area of rain forest and mountain valleys that is partly in Brazil, partly in Venezuela, became headline news around the world in the late 1980s. Hoards of gold miners suddenly descended on their lands, where they had lived in virtual isolation for millennia, their core lands formally designated as a reserve and barred to outsiders. Having been largely spared contact with the outside world, the Yanomami had survived as the largest indigenous tribe in Amazonia, with about 10,000 living in Brazil, and slightly more than that across the border in Venezuela. The miners laid waste Yanomami lands in their search for gold, brushing aside the natives often with appaling brutality. For example, as recently as August 1993 an estimated 40 or more Yanomami were massacred by prospectors, the men being shot while the women were slashed with machetes and some of the children decapitated. The Brazilian attorney general condemned the attack as "genocide."

Despite attempts by the authorities to curb the rapacious prospectors, large portions of the Yanomami reservation have been seized by miners. Their river waters have been poisoned with mercury illegally used in extracting gold, and thousands of Yanomami have succumbed to diseases spread by the invaders. Malaria is rife. The Yanomami, in consequence of the horrors visited upon them, have come to symbolize the plight of the indigenous peoples of Amazonia as a whole.

The Yanomami, whose name means "human beings," live in villages, with each village consisting of a large extended family comprising as many as 400 people. They

live communally in a *shabono*, which is a large circular hut some 25 feet (8 m) high. It is oval in shape, with the palm-thatched roof sloping down to a huge central courtyard. They sleep in hammocks suspended from rafters. These villages are essentially farming communities. Plantain is the staple crop, and when the land can no longer sustain renewed planting they move on and clear another area of forest. This seminomadic existence chimes with their hunting and gathering activities, which add essential protein to their diet. From childhood Yanomamis hunt with bows and arrows tipped with curare, a deadly natural poison they extract from forest plants. Fish as well as birds and animals are prey to these potent weapons.

The Xingu experiment

Of the several large Amerindian reservations in Amazonia, Xingu Indigenous Park is the best known. It was established in the early 1960s through the efforts of the Villas Boas brothers, three celebrated Brazilian anthropologists. During World War II they had become fascinated with the Xinguanos, a tribe living in the upper Xingu region of Brazil. The Xingu is the most easterly of the principal tributaries that join the Amazon from the south, joining the mainstream just 300 miles (480 km) from Belém. But there are tortuous rapids upstream, and in the course of events the upper Xingu and its inhabitants were almost entirely overlooked until the 20th century. This changed when a wartime construction project to link Rio de Janeiro and Manaus by a series of airstrips focused attention on the upper Xingu, which lay on the flight path.

Contact with the Xinguanos prompted the intervention of the Villas Boas brothers, who dedicated themselves to preserving their status and their homelands. It was the brothers' conviction that integration into Brazilian society was not in the interests of tribes that had succeeded in preserving their traditional way of life. Assimilation could only result, they argued, in the loss of cultural identity in return for second-class citizenship within the wider community. The brothers were very persuasive and gained widespread support in influential quarters for their campaign to save the upper Xingu for the Xinguanos.

Once Xingu Indigenous Park was established, the brothers set about persuading both neighboring and distant tribes to enter the sanctuary. Their efforts met with success. Local tribes such as the Suya and Juruna took up residence in the park, and others

Above and opposite: Members of the Xikrin community adorned according to their ancestral traditions. Despite the diversity of the ethnic groups living within Xingu Indigenous Park, some rituals unite all the communities. Two of the most important are the *kwarúp*, a ceremony in honor of a recently deceased tribal chief, which can extend to others who have died recently, and the *yawarí*, which celebrates the ancient dead. After the *kwarúp*, the adolescent boys of the tribe are initiated into the community as men, followed by the adolescent girls. Marriages are also incorporated into these rituals to reinforce the bonds between the various communities.

Above: An example of the craft work of the Xikrin Indians.

such as the Kayabi were transferred there. By the 1990s the park was home to some 3,500 Amerindians from 17 tribes. Most, like the original Xinguanos and the Suya are from the Ge linguistic family, but some like the Juruna and Kayabi are Tupi-speaking. In their original homelands these tribes might have been fierce enemies, but in the park they coexist peacefully enough. Many of these tribes were on the brink of extinction when they resettled, but their numbers have been increasing, in some cases doubling and trebling. For example the Kayabi numbered under 200 when they were resettled in 1966, but within a generation their population grew to over 500.

Despite the overall success of the Xingu Indigenous Park project, it has not been without its frictions and dissatisfactions. As everywhere in Amazonia, there is the enduring pressure of outside interests on the riches of the rain forest. Illegal logging is endemic, and in an incident in 1980 natives attacked and killed 11 loggers. Apart from the fear of encroachment, not all the resettled tribes have been content with their new home. The Panará are the last remaining descendants of the Southern Cayapó, a group of tribes that once dwelt in a large portion of central Brazil. Fierce warriors, the Southern Cayapó put up stiff resistance against the Portuguese invaders, but inevitably they were overpowered, and by the beginning of the 20th century they were thought to be extinct. However, the Panará took refuge in the extreme north of Mato Grosso state in the Peixoto de Azevedo watershed, until they were relocated to the Xingu Indigenous Park in 1975.

The Panará never really settled in. The lands they now farmed were less fertile than those they had left behind, and they blamed this on the fact that it did not contain the bones of their ancestors, which they believed brought fruitfulness to their crops. After prolonged negotiations in the 1990s the Panará were granted an unspoiled portion of their original lands, and nearly half of their total number of 174 set to work building a new village there, the plan being to bring the entire tribe home once the village economy became viable.

The European presence

The arrival of the Europeans was catastrophic for the Amerindians. Europeans, too, gravitated naturally to the floodplain, with the predictable result that, over time, the natives were driven further and further into the depths of the forest.

Today, depending on how they are differentiated, there are perhaps 200 tribes surviving in Amazonia, many of them with tiny populations. As everywhere in the New World the decimation of the native peoples was caused by a combination of displacement, deliberate extermination and the spread of European diseases against which the indigenous peoples had no resistance. In Amazonia, too, slavery continued to take a great toll as recently as the beginning of the 20th century during the final years of the rubber boom.

Because their colonization efforts were focused on Mexico, the Caribbean and the west coast of South America, the Spanish showed only fitful interest in following up Orellana's navigation of the Amazon in the early 1540s (see Chapter 1). Orellana managed to get crown backing for a return expedition to the mouth of the Amazon in 1549, but the enterprise ended in disaster and Orellana's death from malaria. Another Spanish expedition a decade later followed Orellana's route from Peru eastward, in search of El Dorado. It was accompanied by indiscriminate slaughter of indigenous peoples and the eventual murder of the expedition leaders.

In the early 17th century English, French and most determinedly Dutch adventurers and traders attempted to gain a foothold in the region, setting up a number of forts and tobacco plantations. By then, however, the Portuguese had sufficient numbers on the coast of Brazil to remove these challenges relatively easily. With Spain preoccupied elsewhere, the interior of Amazonia came under Portuguese control almost by default. But while getting hold of Amazonia proved easy for the Portuguese, making profitable use of it was a different story.

Despite the undying tales and rumors about Amazonia's fabulous wealth, the truth as experienced by Portuguese settlers could not have been more different. While the plantation system of agriculture never proved feasible, in shabby scattered communities along the river they did manage to grow tobacco, on the backs of Amerindian and some African slave labor. But compared to the great tobacco-growing regions of the Caribbean and, later, such English colonies as Virginia and the Carolinas, Amazonian tobacco output was meager.

With agriculture so problematical, the settlers turned to extractive activities — that is, to stripping their surroundings of whatever had market value. Cacao (chocolate beans) grew wild, as did many spices such as *canela*, a tree-bark with a cinnamon flavor and *cravo*, or "wild clove." Europe provided eager markets for such commodities, as it did for oil extracted from turtle eggs. In the short term this brought income, but the

Above: Woman on Marajó Island, at the mouths of the Amazon and Tocantins rivers. Marajó is one of the largest river islands in the world (around the size of Switzerland), with 250,000 inhabitants and many *fazendas* (ranches or farms).

settlers made no attempt to cultivate plants or domesticate animals in order to harvest them on a sustainable basis. As supplies close to hand disappeared the search spread out further and further afield, which continuously undermined the valuable resources — just the first in the long list of ecological disasters that would be visited upon Amazonia.

A simultaneous ecological and human disaster overwhelmed the Amerindian populations, which got swept up in the process. Slavery and inhumane treatment took their inevitable toll, but even more catastrophic was the introduction of infectious European diseases such as measles, influenza, tuberculosis and, deadliest of all, smallpox. Having neither natural resistance nor any effective treatment, the natives succumbed in huge numbers, as epidemic followed epidemic throughout the 17th and 18th centuries. It is estimated that 40,000 died in a single year during one smallpox epidemic.

With a demoralized population that slowly declined generation upon generation, Amazonia settled into a seemingly permanent torpor, largely unaffected by various failed immigration and development schemes attempted by the colonial authorities. Even the momentous developments of the 1820s, which brought an end to the Spanish and Portuguese empires in South America and established the independent nation states of Peru (1821), Brazil (1822), Bolivia (1825), Colombia, Ecuador and Venezuela (early 1830s), had little effect on Amazonia.

In 1835–36, however, a massive revolt devastated the region around Belém. Called the Cabanagem Rebellion, it became a focus for the despair of Amerindians, mixed-bloods, and slave or dependent blacks. It broke out spontaneously in early 1835, and after several days of savage fighting the surviving Belém authorities fled, leaving the rebels in control. The rebellion took its name from the seething underclass who were called *cabanos* because they lived in cabana huts along the riverbanks and floodplain. Lawlessness afflicted the region around Belém for more than a year. Many factories and businesses were destroyed and their white owners put to death.

The Cabanagem Rebellion was doomed from the start, however. Its leaders declared independence from Brazil but they had no positive program of government and reform, and it was only a matter of time before they fell out amongst themselves. By the time it was suppressed the following year Belém lay in ruins and some 30,000 were dead, more than a fifth of the region's population. By the middle of the 19th century, after 300 years of European efforts to stamp their presence on Amazonia, the region was not only impoverished but largely abandoned.

Opposite: There are still some relics of Amazonia's colonial past to be seen. One of them is the Railroad Museum of Pôrto Velho, which commemorates the unsuccessful Madeira-Mamoré Railroad.

The great rubber boom

It was at this point that rubber entered the scene, to dramatic effect. Right from the beginning Spanish and Portuguese explorers carried home elastic balls that the natives fashioned from gum extracted from the rubber tree. These bouncing balls were just a curiosity, and remained so even after the intrepid Charles-Marie de la Condamine presented the wondrous material to the Academy of Science in Paris in the 18th century. Condamine explained in detail how the latex (he took the term from the Spanish for milk, *leche*) was fashioned by the natives into all sorts of useful objects from galoshes to pumps and even syringes.

However, little by little the properties of rubber came to the attention of inventive minds. The 18th-century English chemist Joseph Priestly discovered that it erased pencil marks, and coined the name "rubber." Then in the 1820s the Scot Charles Mackintosh succeeded in rubberizing cloth to make the first waterproof raincoat. The waterproof property of rubber was also put to use for making foul-weather shoes and boots. Gradually, a modest manufacturing and export industry based on rubber grew up in Belém, but nothing more. For rubber had one serious limitation for its infant new markets in the temperate climates of Europe and North America — it became brittle when cold.

In 1839 a previously unsuccessful American inventor, Charles Goodyear, discovered the process of vulcanization, in which a chemical reaction between rubber and sulfur stabilizes the material's elasticity through a much wider temperature range. Suddenly the applications for rubber began to multiply, and with the development of the pneumatic tire by John Dunlop, another Scot, in the 1880s, the demand for the versatile material became insatiable. First the bicycle and then the automobile devoured all the rubber Amazonia could supply. At the same time, rubber's insulating properties meant that it had unlimited application for the electrical revolution that was getting into full swing.

In the closing decades of the 19th century Amazonia was in the throes of a "black gold" rush, every bit as frenetic as any of the gold rushes that enlivened the same period. It was centered on Manaus in the heart of Brazilian Amazonia, where the precious rubber trees grew in profusion. But Peru, Colombia and Bolivia all shared in the bonanza. Brazilian exports, which had been negligible in the 1820s, were in excess of 6,000 tons by 1870, peaking at 45,000 tons in 1911. Enormous fortunes were made

by the lucky, ruthless few who gained control of the industry, while over 100,000 mainly migrant laborers from northeastern Brazil toiled in the forest collecting the precious latex. Trading settlements sprang up throughout the interior and the shipping ports of Belém, Iquitos and above all Manaus became fabulously rich.

Luxurious hotels and restaurants lined elegant new boulevards, along with high-class bordellos and other venues for grand and gaudy entertainments imported from Europe. Most famously, a magnificent opera house — Teatro Amazonas — was built in Manaus, with materials and skilled craftsmen transported all the way from Europe to the middle of Amazonia without regard to cost. The burgeoning class of super rich even indulged in the luxury of sending their laundry to Europe. As fast as fortunes were squandered, more fortunes were made.

With Amazonia enjoying an almost total monopoly on the commodity and demand showing no sign of peaking let alone abating, it seemed that the good times

A rubber tapper (above left) making a new incision on a rubber tree. The bark is crisscrossed with earlier cuts, and latex is extracted in much the same way that sap is taken from the sugar maple tree to make maple syrup. A diagonal incision in the bark allows the sap (the latex) to flow.
A metal container is affixed at the end of the cut to collect the latex (above center). The rubber tapper periodically collects the contents of the container and makes a further incision in the bark.

Above right: After the white liquid is extracted from the tree, firewood is needed for smoking and processing the rubber.

would roll forever. Then, almost overnight, the rubber boom collapsed. The seeds of its destruction were literally being sown at the very height of the boom, in British Malaya. In the 1880s the English planter Henry Wickham succeeded in smuggling seeds and saplings of the rubber tree out of Manaus to the Royal Botanical Gardens at Kew. After being nurtured at Kew, specimens were dispatched to British possessions in southeast Asia, where conditions were thought suitable for cultivation.

The ploy worked spectacularly, and by 1902 plantation-grown Malayan rubber began coming on the market. It was in some ways inferior to the wild rubber from which it was derived, but much cheaper, and within a decade rubber from Malayan and other Southeast Asian plantations overhauled Amazonia in terms of production. The dislocations caused by World War I (1914–18) further depressed Amazonia's rubber industry, and throughout the 1920s the downward spiral continued apace.

The boomtowns became deserted, the fine buildings derelict, the dwindling population impoverished. There was a brief resurgence in Brazilian rubber during World War II when Far Eastern supplies fell under Japanese occupation, but that did not stem the long-term decline of what today is a comparatively minor industry employing a few thousand workers.

The recent wave of immigration

The brief resurgence of the rubber industry in the 1940s brought a new wave of immigrants from Brazil's impoverished northeast. The 1970s was the era of "big projects" and the federal government's implementation of its "Project for National Integration" was aimed at populating the region. A highway system was created, together with new agricultural projects, to establish new towns and bring in settlers from all over the country. Other countries were also trying to populate the regions of Amazonia within their borders to strengthen their claims to sovriegnty.

During the closing decades of the 20th century, the various nations with a substantial stake in Amazonia encouraged much greater use of its resources, and this has entailed an enormous migration into the region. The major towns and cities have mushroomed in size, roads have knifed through previously virgin rain forest, and massive mining projects have devastated huge tracts of land. All this activity has brought wave after wave of hopeful settlers from the poorer regions, particularly from overcrowded southern Brazil. Many of these are farmers descended from immigrants from southern and eastern Europe as well as Japan and Korea, adding to Amazonia's rich ethnic diversity. Government colonization schemes were primarily intended to provide opportunities for small-scale farmers, many of whom failed in the demanding conditions of Amazonia and moved on to more distant frontiers or gravitated to towns. But many others made a success of their small farms along the pioneer highways, and have created sustainable pasture land and crops.

The Carajas Mining Project established a line of development from southern Pará to the city of São Luís in the state of Maranhão, as rail and road networks were constructed to take the iron ore and other minerals from the forest to the port at São Luís. The logging industry is another that still promotes the settlement of new migrants into Amazonia. At present the population of Amazonian Brazil is around 20 million.

Opposite: A *caboclo* family. The term *caboclo* refers to local people who live along the riverways, eking out a living by fishing, turtle-hunting, and wherever they can fit into the ecotourism industry. The *caboclos* constitute the axis of the community that populates Amazonia, and integrate different customs, clothing and dwellings. Some are Amerindians, others are poor whites or blacks. *Caboclo* is used as an insult by urban dwellers who disparage the river folk, dismissing them as rustic and backward.

CHAPTER SIX
The Cultural Heritage

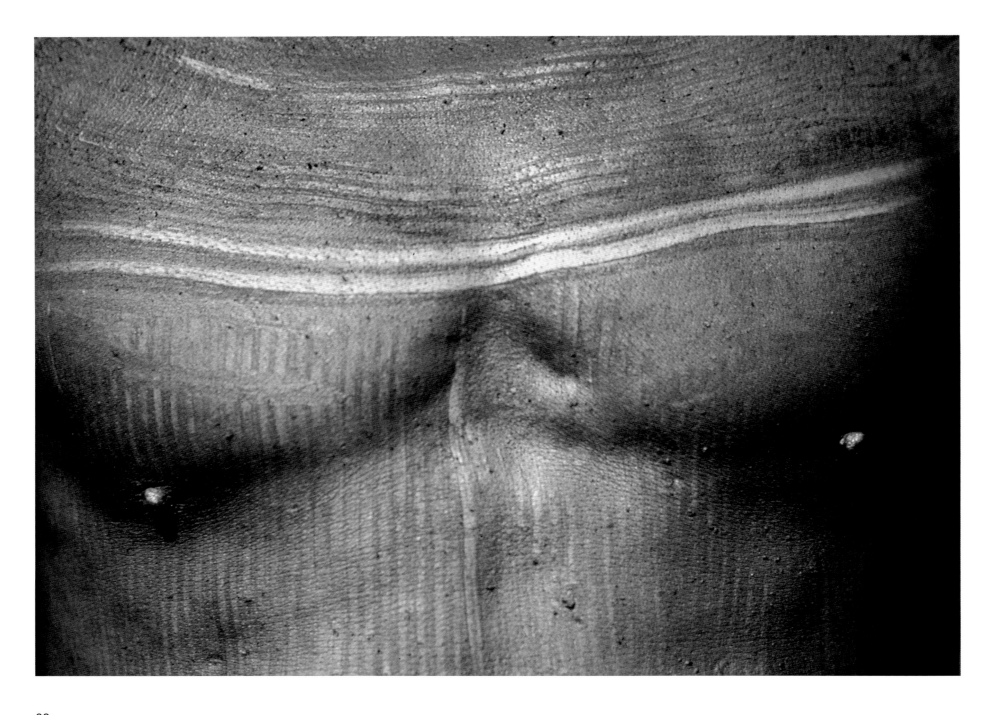

A world of rich cultural traditions

There are as many Amerindian cultures in Amazonia, with their attendant myths and beliefs, as there are tribes. All but the most fundamental generalizations can therefore be misleading. However, central to the thinking of indigenous Amazonians is animism — the belief that all living things — animals and plants as well as humans — have spirits. All these spirits, of the dead as well as the living, interact according to complex hierarchies and in response to the ever-changing situations of life.

Some spirits are good, others evil, and placating dangerous or evil spirits is an important part of ritual life. Illnesses are attributed to malevolent spirits, recovery from illness and safe delivery of children to benevolent spirits. Leading and overseeing the ceremonial dances, songs and incantations aimed at placating the spirit world is the shaman, who is both a spiritual healer and defender of the tribe from its enemies — since he can enlist the aid of powerful spirits. Commonly the shaman wields his powers while under the influence of hallucinatory drugs, which brings him into closer communion with the spirit world.

The rites of birth, puberty and death are accompanied by a variety of ceremonies that reflect the spiritual views of the tribe. Burial is common, but the Yanomami cremate their dead and then later consume the ashes in order that the dead shall live through

Above and opposite: Festivals and ceremonies are a time when traditional dress, body painting and adornment link the cultural heritage of the past with the people of today.

Pages 96–97: A traditional hunting bow and arrow of the Yanomami.
Page 97: The most sophisticated ceramic artifacts in the Amazon have been found on Marájo Island. Traditionally decorated in vibrant red, black and white, these ceramics form part of the rich cultural tradition that continues today in the production of hand-painted vases, pots and urns.

them — another example of the powerful guiding force of animism within their lives.

The animistic view of existence comes naturally to people who live as intimately with nature as the Amazonians do, and this sense of being at one with nature is reflected in daily life, which is carefully regulated according to the demands imposed by the natural world. As a rule tasks are clearly defined between the sexes, with men responsible for hunting, fishing and warfare, women for tending crops, cooking and other domestic chores, and for looking after children.

Myths and legends

Amazonia is rich in legend and myth, all specific to the region and inspired by animistic beliefs, but one myth in particular resonates beyond the Amazon and may reflect a fleeting contact with Christian teaching at some stage. Jurupari was conceived by the virgin Ceuci, as a result of her eating a particularly succulent sweet fruit covered with hairs. In recognition of his supernatural origins, the sun god, the creator of life, charged Jurupari with redeeming the human race, which had strayed from the original paths of goodness. In addition, Jurupari was to make the rounds of the villages looking for a perfect bride for the sun god.

In the course of his travels Jurupari curbed injustices and re-established harmony, while at the same time introducing initiation rites for young men and women. This involved masks, musical processions and harsh physical ordeals to prepare youth for adult life. Despite introducing these enduring practices, Jurupari was unable to find the perfect bride for the sun god, and so his pilgrimage continues. Until he succeeds, there can be no marriage between heaven and earth. That is why women beautify themselves with feathers and the vibrant red and blue-black dyes that are characteristic adornments throughout the Amazon region. They are hoping to be chosen as the sun god's bride. When that happy day arrives, Jurupari will have completed his mission and can return to heaven to take his place with the sun god, and humanity will once again be at one with its creator.

Opposite and above: The startling colours of the rain forest are reflected in the body ornamentation of the indigenous peoples of Amazonia. Although modern dyes and materials have been incorporated into traditional adornments, the brilliant feathers of the rain forest birds are still used. Both of the headpieces are of the Xikrin people.

Above: The great snake, sucuri, is a popular subject for Amazonian legends — traditional and modern.

Opposite: River dolphins, like much of the fauna of the Amazon, are under threat. Here, a startlingly pink dolphin has been captured as part of a research program to discover more about the behaviour of this remarkable animal.

Boto the Seducer

The freshwater pink dolphin which cruises slowly along the bottom of some Amazonian rivers is not the human-friendly playmate that his sea-going cousin is, and this surfaces in a number of myths that have a sting in the tail. It is sometimes called Boto (dolphin) and sometimes Bufeo Colorado (the dolphin's Latin name, which translates into English as "funny color," an allusion to its pinkish hue caused by its having blood vessels just under the skin's surface). From time to time Boto emerges from his watery home in the guise of a handsome young man. He is always exquisitely dressed in a white suit, but he has the peculiar sartorial habit of not removing his hat under any circumstances. It is said that if a person creeps up on Boto while he is sleeping and peeks under the hat the reason is revealed — human in all other respects, Boto retains a blow-hole on the top of his head.

Boto is bent on a predictable mission. He turns up at parties, where he is the life and soul and seduces pretty girls. The cad always departs before dawn, and if he is followed he can be seen diving into the river, where he resumes his dolphin form. If he lures a human into the water that person becomes so enchanted that he or she never returns to land. As for the victims of his seduction, they give birth to "children of the Boto," as children of unknown fathers are sometimes called. Should there be any doubt, it is a simple matter to examine the baby's head, where the fontanelle confirms its Boto parentage!

The Great Snake

Not surprisingly the giant anaconda has entered mythology as a fearsome foe of humanity. According to the story, there was once a malevolent woman so vile that she even ate children. To put a stop to her predations the villagers hurled her into the river. Unfortunately, instead of being drowned the wicked witch was saved by an evil spirit in the water, who fathered a child by her. The boy was transformed into a snake so that it could live in the river.

The man-snake grew to such an enormous size that it devoured all the fish and then invaded the land in search of more prey, human as well as animal. In stormy weather the Great Snake slithers back into the water, leaving furrows on the ground that fill up as streams. As it swims along the river it leaves cascades in its wake, but what is most terrifying are its enormous luminous eyes, like lanterns. Fishermen in their canoes keep a keen lookout so that they can flee from those baleful eyes.

Above and opposite: The paintings on the bodies of women, children and old people, as well as the multicolored ornaments, are essential in retelling and celebrating the indigenous myths.

Caipora, Protector of Animals

Sometimes called Curupira, Caipora can assume a variety of shapes, but most commonly appears as a handsome young boy. He is a mischievous as well as benevolent being, walking with his feet backwards to bamboozle hunters. Caipora's mission is to protect nature, especially animals from hunters who kill needlessly. If they suspect his presence hunters may create a smokescreen (literally) to ward off Caipora's vengeance. Performing a similar role in protecting endangered animals is the Anhangá, an Amazonian goblin. Hunters who kill young animals, such as birds in the nest, or pregnant females, are in danger of Anhangá's wrath, which takes the form of infecting them with a terrible fever that drives them insane.

Yara, the Mother of Waters

From the beginning of the colonial period native women, who were prized for their beauty and good nature, were objects of desire for the conquering Portuguese and Spanish. From encounters between the two, sometimes consensual, often violent, came the intermingling of races that is so conspicuous today. There also arose legends about the initial encounters, such as the story of the beautiful Yara.

Yara was much courted by the young men of her tribe, but she paid them no heed as she bathed in the clear waters of the river, oblivious to their attentions. One fateful day she was accosted by a group of white intruders, who raped her by the water's edge. Out of pity, the spirit of the waters received her battered body and infused it with renewed life, strength and beauty. However, to ensure that she never would suffer a similar indignity the spirit transformed Yara into a mermaid.

Men continued to be fascinated by her beauty, but as they fell under her spell and jumped into the river to clutch her they were drawn into the watery depths never to return.

The legend of Manioc

Manioc, a thick starchy root used to make flour, is by far the most important staple for most Amazonian tribes. It has a most touching mythical origin. Long ago the daughter of a native chieftain was expelled from her village because she was unaccountably pregnant. Isolated in an old hut, the girl received food from relatives and so eventually gave birth — to a very white, beautiful boy whom she called Mani. When news of the remarkable looking Mani seeped back to the village the chief's heart was softened and

Above and opposite: Scenes from the annual Boi-Bumbá festival, where indigenous and colonial traditions combine in vibrant celebrations.

he restored his daughter to her rightful position. Little Mani was beloved of all. Then tragedy befell. Displaying no symptoms of illness, Mani suddenly died at the age of three. His mother buried him close to her house and wept copiously over his grave. Eventually, through her tears she saw the first shoots of a little plant growing out of the grave. The villagers all gathered around to witness the miracle of this unknown plant, which had strong white roots in the shape of a horn. They sampled the plant and pronounced it good. They named it *mandioca* or manioc, the last part of the name meaning horn-shaped. So was born the plant that has sustained Amazonian life since time immemorial.

The song of ill omen

The common potoo is a nocturnal bird with an unmistakable, mournful call that is considered a bad omen. But it was not always so with the potoo, which once had the most beautiful song in the forest, the envy of all other birds. One day the potoo fell in love with the shimmering full moon and flew at once to the highest branch of the tallest tree in the forest to serenade his new love. Getting no response, the bird flew up and up toward the object of his desire, until eventually he exhausted himself and came crashing back to earth. The impact with the ground knocked the poor bird half senseless, but as his head began to clear he quickly tried to recover his voice. Tragically, the once melodious notes were no more, and in their place that eerie scream that can be heard mainly on moonlit nights.

Boi-Bumbá

The Boi-Bumbá is the best known folk festival in Amazonia, and the festivities reach their peak in the city of Parintins, in Amazonas state, at the end of June. The celebrations are built around the legend of a *caboclo* (someone of mixed indigenous and Caucasian ancestry) who kills one of the oxen on his employer's *fazenda* (ranch) to satisfy the cravings of his pregnant wife. When his boss finds out about the deed he orders the *caboclo* to bring the beast back to life. To do this, the *caboclo* seeks the help

Above: A native craft exhibit at Boa Vista, a planned city and the state capital of Roraima — a remote and beautiful region on the border of Brazil and Venezuela.

of a *pajé*, or healer, from a local tribe. The ox comes back to life and the people celebrate by dancing around the animal with the *caboclo*, who is forgiven by his employer. Combining music, theater, drums and dancing, the festival is watched by tens of thousands, as it celebrates this and many other Amazonian legends.

Gifts to the world

Beyond such endearing myths and legends, the indigenous peoples of Amazonia have contributed much to the wider world. This is most conspicuous in the nations that include large portions of Amazonia within their borders. For example many placenames in Brazil have an indigenous origin, and most fruit, fish and forest animals are known by their Amerindian names. Manioc flour is a natural part of the diet throughout the country, and guaraná drinks are not just a big hit there but have a following all over the world. And there has never been a more comfortable device for sleeping safely off the ground than a hammock, which can be seen everywhere throughout Amazonia.

A potentially much larger gift to the world has still to be fully accepted. The Amazon rain forest is sometimes referred to as a huge pharmacy, and it is the indigenous peoples who discovered over time the wondrous uses to which unique barks, leaves and roots could be put. Quinine, until recently the main weapon to ward off malaria, is a product of the Amazon, and curare is widely used as a muscle relaxant in the developed world. These are just two well-known examples of potent medical drugs that have come out of the Amazonian rain forest, and further exploiting this natural resource will be a significant aspect of sustainable development there. The indigenous peoples have much to contribute to this important enterprise.

The concept of sustainable development is particularly relevant to Amerindians, since it is the only avenue that will enable them to improve their standard of living while retaining more than a semblance of cultural identity and integrity. It would be naive and patronizing to expect the peoples of the Amazon to continue to live without modern benefits where they can be obtained — medicines, various tools to reduce drudgery, education for their children, and so on. Sustainable development in this context means enabling the inhabitants to make a decent living from the harvesting of rain forest products on a renewable basis, that is, without the destruction of the forest itself. As well as medicinal plants, such products include the raw materials for various arts and crafts that can be marketed to tourists, for example, plant fibers and dyes, canoe paddles, and other wood carvings and artifacts. Woodworking is particularly significant because of the availability of valuable hardwoods for which Amazonia is famous. The wholesale felling and exportation of coveted hardwoods is the antithesis of sustainable development; highly skilled woodworking, which involves adding considerable value to relatively small amounts of the raw material, is perfectly sustainable. Adding value to timber products at the community level also increases the incentive to conserve the forest as a source of continuing income — while making less attractive the idea of selling off timber rights to outside interests.

Perhaps most significant of all, however, the surviving Amazonian tribes reflect an aspect of the human predicament that has great and growing relevance for the rest of the human race — the need to exist in some sort of harmony with the natural world. That is why the fate of Amazonia and its inhabitants has come to exert such a powerful hold on the imagination of people, especially young people, everywhere.

Above: Sunset on the waters of the Madeira River.

CHAPTER SEVEN
The Cities

Amazonia's principal cities

Naturally enough, the main urban centers of Amazonia are located along the mighty river itself. With the exception of Iquitos in Peru, the most significant both historically and commercially are in Brazil, where Amazonia makes up 42 percent of the country. The region is only lightly populated, with few good roads, so it is the Amazon and its tributaries that form the network for transportation and communication, as they have done for centuries. Europeans used the rivers to explore and colonize Amazonia, establishing settlements at strategic points on the river. In approximate geographical order from the east coast of Brazil, the main centers are Belém, Macapá, Pôrto Velho, Manaus and Iquitos.

Belém

Belém, situated on the southern bank of the Amazon estuary, is the gateway to Brazilian Amazonia. The capital of the state of Pará, it has a population of almost 1.3 million. It was founded by the Portuguese in 1616 and given the name City of Our Lady of Bethlehem (Belém). Its original role was to protect the mouth of the river from any

Above: The bustling Ver-o-Peso Market, Belém.

Opposite: The Cathedral Square, in Belém, shows clearly the influence of Portuguese architecture.

Pages 110–111: The port of Manaus boomed during the Rubber Cycle at the end of the 19th century, and is still the major city on the river today.
Page 111: The façade of the church of Saint Alexander, Belém.

Above: In the foreground is part of the Emílio Goeldi Museum in Belém. Founded in 1866, it has been an important center for research into Amazonia's natural history and the history of its people. The zoological park is one of the finest zoos in South America and the botanical gardens and archaeological displays hold fine collections.

rivals, and to facilitate the colonizing of an Amazonian empire. It rapidly established itself as the main port for trading in Amerindian slaves and for exporting cacao and other Amazonian produce, such as vanilla, cinnamon, indigo and turtle shells. It is still the biggest port on the Amazon, where 56 percent of all cargo shipped out is timber.

After some initial success, Belém started to decline as the slave labor force taken from the surrounding rain forest dwindled through death and disease. By the 1820s and 1830s it was in an abject condition. When the Cabanagem Rebellion in the middle 1830s left Belém in ruins, it seemed destined to sink into oblivion.

Then, as if by a miracle, the rubber boom began in the 1850s, utterly transforming Belém's fortunes. At its peak half a century later Belém was a very prosperous city by any standards, and the principal exporter of Brazilian rubber. Like Manaus a thousand miles (1,600 km) upstream, Belém refashioned itself along glamorous European lines, with elegant plazas and avenues, where the newly rich paraded themselves in their Parisian finery. The neoclassical Teatro da Paz is almost on par with the Manaus Teatro Amazonas, and many of Europe's most celebrated stars sang and danced there, including Anna Pavlova.

The collapse of the Brazilian rubber industry that coincided with the beginning of World War I in 1914 hit Belém hard, but it was able to keep going because of the growing market for rain forest timber, initially for domestic consumption but in recent decades as a major export commodity. The construction of the Belém-Brasilia Highway and financial incentives for industry also helped to strengthen the economy.

The bustling port is also the jumping off point for nature sightseeing on nearby Marajó Island. This enormous island, the result of eons of silt and sand building up in the estuary, is noteworthy for its huge herds of water buffalo that are ranched there. It also has an abundance of wildlife, in particular birds and monkeys.

Above: The neoclassical façade of the Teatro da Paz (Theatre of Peace) in Belém. Constructed between 1868 and 1874, it is a superb example of the wealth of the city during the rubber boom.

Left: Another view of Ver-o-Peso Market, with the clock of the central square. In the background are the iron towers of the Mercado de Ferro, which houses part of the fish section of the market. The iron framework for the building was shipped out in sections from England and assembled in Belém.

Above: The port of Santana, 15 miles (25 km) southwest of Macapá, through which the entire production of manganese of the region goes out.

Left: The fort of São José, in Macapá, replaced the old fort of Santo Antonio, around which the city gathered. Built by the Portuguese between 1764 and 1782 to defend the north side of the Amazon from the French, the fort constitutes one of the most beautiful military monuments of Amazonia today.

Apart from the splendid Teatro, Belém is noteworthy for the old Ver-o-Peso Market, originally a slave market but now crammed with fish, fruit and vegetables along with nuts and medicinal herbs from the rain forest. The Emílio Goeldi Museum is another major attraction. It is a combination of museum and zoological gardens. The museum has an excellent collection of Amerindian artifacts, including beautiful ceramics, some of which are up to 5,000 years old. The zoological gardens comprises a zoo, aquarium and aviary and ranks among the best in South America.

Macapá

Across the estuary from Belém, on the north bank, is the city of Macapá, capital of the state of Amapá. Amapá is a poor region, and most of its inhabitants live in the capital, originally a rubber town, but today largely dependent upon manganese and, to a lesser extent, timber.

Macapá lies on the Equator and has a population of around 270,000. It grew around the site of an old English fort built in the early 17th century but quickly captured by the Portuguese in their successful campaign to drive the English and Dutch out of the Amazon region.

Pôrto Velho

Pôrto Velho is the capital of the Brazilian state of Rondônia, on the great Madeira River in western Amazonia. Great things were forecast for Pôrto Velho when it was established in the early years of the 20th century as the terminus for the Madeira–Mamoré Railroad, hacked through the forest to bring Bolivian rubber to the Madeira, from where it could be easily transported to Manaus and onward to the waiting world. With unimaginably bad timing the railroad was completed in 1912, just as the rubber boom was about to collapse. Pôrto Velho remained a sleepy backwater until the 1980s, when gold prospectors descended on it in droves, and today, while the gold fever has abated, the city has a population of 350,000. Pôrto Velho is both state capital and the regional hub from which the agricultural produce of western Brazil is shipped out to domestic and foreign markets. It has seen considerable growth in cargo volume, mainly due to the

Above: Macapá, capital of the state of Amapá, is located on the northern banks of the Amazon River and constitutes an important commercial center. The capital is also crossed by the line of the Equator; a milestone indicates exactly where the imaginary line goes through.

Above: Ships take tourists and locals along the waters of the Madeira River, near Pôrto Velho, Rondônia. The city, built as a consequence of the construction of the Madeira-Mamoré Railroad, received a lot of English railroad workers, who influenced its architecture, as can be observed in the church and house right.

large increase in soybean production in Rondônia and the neighboring state of Mato Grosso. Industrial expansion too has been made possible by the use of natural gas for thermal power generation.

Further west from Pôrto Velho is the town of Rio Branco, which also arose in the wake of the rubber boom. It was established around a rubber extraction plant, founded in 1882, near the Acre River. Today it is the state capital of Acre, the smallest Brazilian state. It does, however, still have 93 percent of its original rain forest, thanks to the efforts of the traditional rubber tappers who resisted the activities of the loggers and ranchers in the region in the 1970s. The charismatic leader of this resistance, Chico Mendes, was assassinated in 1988 and his death served to focus international attention on the plight of the forest. A park near the town is a memorial to his achievements with native forest, wildlife and theme huts displaying the various aspects of life in the area. Today the town's main ecomonic activities are food production, timber and furniture.

Manaus – commercial hub of Amazonia and ecotourism center

Manaus, the capital of the state of Amazonas, is the largest and best known city in Amazonia. Founded in the 17th century on the north bank of the Rio Negro, just above its confluence with the mainstream, Manaus owes its fame to the rubber boom, which in its extravagant heyday it came to symbolize. Indeed Manaus became a byword for the excesses of its *nouveau riche* society. The glitzy opera house, its enduring symbol, was almost entirely built and furbished with the finest Europe could provide: its iron skeleton brought from Scotland, the fantastic white cupola comprising 36,000 tiles shipped over from Alsace, chandeliers of Italian crystal and French bronze, everywhere the finest Italian marble and stone. For the grand opening in 1896 an Italian opera company performed Ponchielli's *La Gioconda*.

This was the apogee of Manaus's golden age, when electric trolleys trundled along its leafy, Parisian-style avenues, where grand palaces and villas boasted telephones and electric lighting, and everyday transactions were commonly conducted with gold coinage and English pounds. A huge floating docks complex was built by the British in 1902 to accommodate the seasonal variations in water level, and it is still a feature of the city.

The opera house was one of the first victims of the slump in rubber exports, clos-

Above: A view of the park in Rio Branco dedicated to the memory of Chico Mendes.

ing in 1912 and becoming derelict and overgrown before it was restored to its former glory in the 1970s. The rest of glamorous Manaus followed suit, and it was not until 1967, when it was granted tax free status (like a free port), that its fortunes began to recover. The so-called Manaus Free Zone is an area of about 4,000 square miles (10,000 sq km) centered on the city. One of four free trade zones in Brazil, the MFZ has from the beginning forged ahead of the others and of the nation as a whole. By the end of the 20th century it was generating over $13 billion a year in industrial production. This has allowed Manaus to reinvent itself as a prosperous commercial and manufacturing center with a population of over 1.5 million. As a consequence of the MFZ it boasts a huge electronics and domestic appliance industry, accounting for 80 percent of all Brazilian audio equipment manufacture, for example, and a staggering 99 percent of all VCR manufacture.

Also, Manaus is the center of ecotourism in Amazonia. River excursions take in a wide variety of the flora and fauna that make Amazonia such an increasingly popular destination. One-day trips usually include the famous meeting of the waters, a few miles downstream from Manaus, where the white and black waters of the mainstream and the Rio Negro run side by side. Longer trips of a few days — and up to a couple of weeks — are still mainly waterborne, and include such attractions as the Anavilhanas Archipelago made up of some 400 islands, 120 miles (192 km) up the Negro.

Other popular tourist destinations along the Rio Negro include Presidente Figueiredo, almost 70 miles (112 km) from Manaus. Sited amidst open forest, the town has over one hundred waterfalls nearby and is called the city of "cascades and caverns." One of the most striking is the Cachoeira da Neblina at 125 feet (35 m). There are also many caverns, including the Caverna de Maroaga, with an entrance almost 71 feet (20 m) high and an interior reaching back 1722 feet (480 m).

Barcelos, about 250 miles (400 km) upriver, is located on the largest fluvial archipelago in the world, Mariuá. This tangle of 1,266 forest-covered islands is an area of indescribable beauty.

Above: Transport by boat is the most popular way for locals and tourists to get around Manaus.

Opposite: An aerial view of Manaus, on the banks of the Rio Negro.

Left: A view of the Floating Dock opened in 1902. Designed by the British it rises and falls with seasonal water levels and at the time was considered a feat of engineering. At the entrance to the dock is the *alfândega* or custom house (above), imported from the U.K. in prefabricated blocks in 1906.

Opposite: The imposing Teatro Amazonas, built with materials imported from Europe during the period of the rubber boom in the 19th century. The theater opened its doors in 1896, and today, totally restored, it still attracts visitors to admire its beauty.

Another 250 miles (400 km) further up the Rio Negro is São Gabriel da Cachoeira, near the border with Colombia and Venezuela. The first European inhabitants were Carmelite brothers who came to convert the indigenous peoples of the area. Today, the town is the point of departure for tourists visiting the Pico da Neblina National Park. There are also tours of the surrounding forest, wetlands and rivers.

Opposite and above left and right: The wealth provided by the rubber boom molded the elaborate architecture that can still be appreciated in Manaus today, such as the Mercado Municipal, above left.

Iquitos

Iquitos in northwestern Peru is the third city of Amazonia, after Manaus and Belém. It has no road links with the outside world, but is readily accessible by water and air. Iquitos was founded as a Jesuit mission in the 18th century, but like Belém and Manaus it was put on the map by the rubber boom. Like them, Iquitos masqueraded as an opulent European city during its salad days, and then slumped back into disrepair during the 20th century. However, oil, timber and ecotourism have in recent years restored much of Iquitos's prosperity and it is a thriving city with a population of over 600,000, the fourth largest in Peru.

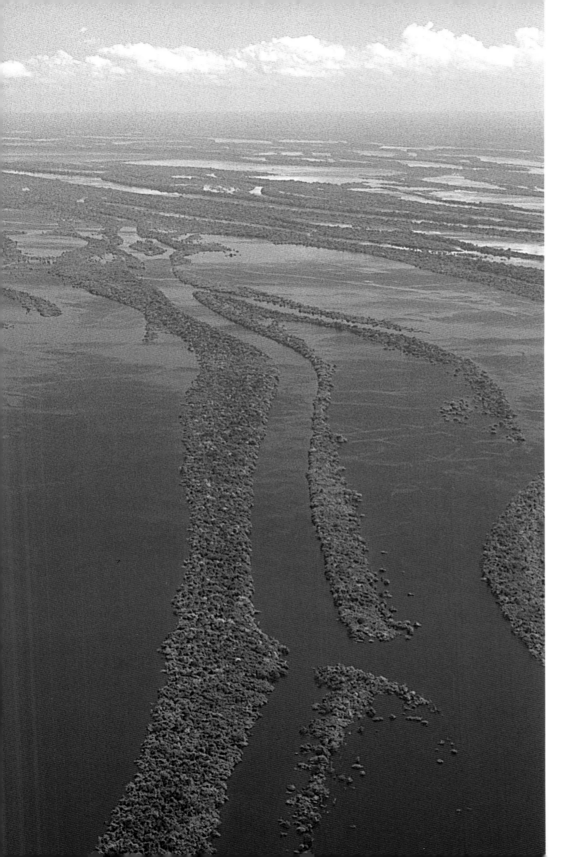

CHAPTER EIGHT
The Present

Above: Almost 13 percent of the native forest in Brazilian Amazonia has already been devastated to make room for grazing lands and cultivations. This frightening percentage means that the forest has lost an area equivalent to the territory of France.

Opposite: A camp in the middle of the rain forest, part of the huge Carajas mining project in north-east Amazonia.

Counting the cost of deforestation

The carefree exploitation of Amazonia's rubber resources came at little or no environmental cost, since it amounted to what today is described as sustainable use — that is, on the whole the latex was gathered without harming the rubber trees, and there was no need to level vast acreages of rain forest in order to get it to the rivers for transporting onwards. A sustainable rubber industry continues today, although in greatly reduced scale from the boom times. But subsequent (and current) attempts to exploit other resources of Amazonia have been anything but cost free in environmental terms.

It is easy to overlook the fact that environmentalism, whether viewed as a movement or simply as an attitude of mind, is a very recent development. In the 1960s, when the various stakeholders in Amazonia began making serious attempts to tap into its potential wealth, their ambition was widely applauded in the developed world, from which there was ample funding. Brazil in particular, which has by far the biggest stake in the region, was seen to be making up for lost time with a string of ambitious projects.

The process began, logically, with road-building to connect the interior, and its mineral and timber resources, with the major conurbations to the south of Amazonia. Two huge projects were undertaken, the Transamazon Highway intended to carve a path right across Amazonia from Belém almost to the Peruvian border, and the

Pages 126–127: The Amazonian floodplains.
Page 127: Harvesting rice.

Belém–Brasilia Highway, connecting the Amazon port with the country's proud new capital, a distance of 1,300 miles (2,100 km). The latter was successfully in operation by the beginning of the 1960s, and more than any other factor was responsible for the surge of interest in Amazonian timber that has left such deep scars on the rain forest.

The Transamazon Highway was even more ambitious, and along with the Great Wall of China is often cited as being visible from space (alone among human constructions). Of the two, the ancient wall is in much the better state of repair. The Transamazon Highway petered out well short of its destination, and by the end of the 20th century large stretches of it were potholed, had been left unpaved or were in a state of total dilapidation. In some ways it was like its inauspicious predecessor, the Madeira–Mamoré Railroad, which was built at the height of the rubber boom and completed just as it ended on the eve of World War I. The construction of the railroad cost thousands of lives, mainly victims of malaria, and all to no purpose as the line was abandoned.

Such big highway projects themselves took a toll on the rain forest through which they sliced, but nothing compared with the activities their construction facilitated. For their purpose was not just to link disparate parts of the country but to bring people and capital right into the the heart of Amazonia, for how could its wealth be tapped without investment and plentiful labor? Successive governments encouraged the clearing of rain forest for big mining and hydroelectric projects as well as huge cattle ranches. Cattle ranchers got big fiscal incentives to cut down mature forest to create artificial pasture land, planted with imported species of suitable grass. A huge "grass rush" occurred in eastern and southern Amazonia, with some 40,000 square miles (100,000 sq km) of forest felled and planted by the mid-1970s.

At the same time settlers were enticed to take advantage of the increasing stretches of deforested land near the roads, and they came in large numbers. Before long it became apparent that the poor Amazonian soil could not support conventional agriculture for any length of time, but that did not stop the influx of hopefuls, who often drifted on from one depleted area to another, and into the towns and cities that were springing up to provide support and infrastructure for all the activity. Itinerant farmers were joined by gold-hungry prospectors in the 1980s, to give a restless almost Wild West flavor to this last American frontier.

Above: A huge open-cast iron ore mine, part of the Carajas project in Pará.

Opposite: Large tracts of rain forest have been cleared for agriculture — some sustainable and some not. The main crops grown on the cleared land include rice (left), maize (top and bottom right) and wheat.

Pages 132–133: The Gran Carajás Project covers a vast area of the state of Pará and is a network of open-cast mines, smelters, railroads and highways.

The Gran Carajás and Calha Norte Projects

Road-building and deforestation have also figured largely in two gigantic enterprises that typify the economic and political forces ranged against the interests of the rain forest. In 1968, a geological survey team in the Carajás range in southern Pará stumbled upon a hill almost entirely made up of high grade iron ore. The Carajás iron ore reserves have been estimated at 18 billion tons, making them the largest in the world. Further exploration uncovered rich deposits of gold, manganese, bauxite and copper. The upshot of these discoveries was the Gran (Greater) Carajás Project, a sprawling mining complex that also includes processing plants and transport links to the coast, along with

all the infrastructure needed to support such a colossal enterprise in the middle of the rain forest. The project's energy demands have led to the construction of dams for the generation of hydroelectric power. This in turn has resulted in the flooding of forests and dislocation of indigenous tribes. In all, Gran Carajás extended its tentacles over an area of some 350,000 square miles (900,000 sq km). It has come under fierce attack from environmentalists both in Brazil and abroad for its high-handed conduct — often employing quasi-military force to ride roughshod over any opposition.

Direct military force has been a significant feature of yet another huge Brazilian project, the Calha Norte (Northern Headquarters). This started up in 1985, under the auspices of the army. The idea was to strengthen national defenses by populating the

Above: Chico Mendes Park near Rio Branco, Acre. This remote state has seen less rain forest destruction than many parts of the Amazon and one-third of its rain forest is either protected or indigenous land — an important resource for future tourism to the area.

remote northern boundaries primarily with Venezuela and Colombia. Effectively this was to put about 4,000 miles (6,400 km) of Brazil's border regions under military jurisdiction. It took the typical form of airstrips, garrisons, roads and civilian settlements to provide amenities and general infrastructure. The Calha Norte Project has proceeded by fits and starts, and at great financial cost. It was widely scorned in the late 1980s and early 1990s because of its cavalier treatment of the Yanomami tribe whose lands it usurped. And the army proved far from even-handed when gold prospectors flooded into Yanomami territory and met resistance. The gun-toting *garimpeiros* were just the sort of tough frontier types that Calha Norte wanted to populate their settlements.

More recently, under the blanket development program called Brazil on the Move, there have been schemes to step up road construction, railroad building, lay gas pipelines through Amazonia, and to develop oil refineries. Three so-called development corridors would link Manaus with the Caribbean through Guyana and Venezuela, the upper Amazon with the Atlantic, and southern Brazil with the Pacific via Bolivia, Peru and Chile. Projects on such a scale are far beyond Brazil's purse — Brazil is one of the world's largest debtor nations — and so require huge foreign investment, and it is at the sharp end of international finance that so much environmentalist lobbying is focused.

The sums involved are colossal. Brazil on the Move envisages a $45 billion investment by 2007 in infrastructure projects to boost the agribusiness, mining and timber sectors. By contrast, the largest of the domestic and international initiatives to promote rain forest conservation and sustainable development is the program of the G-7 nations. It is funded to the tune of $340 million.

In January 2001, the authoritative journal *Science* carried a report on findings by the Smithsonian Tropical Research Institute (STRI) based in Panama. It was written by William F. Laurance, a scientist with the joint U.S.–Brazil research team, and it attempted to bring an overarching perspective to Brazil on the Move. Working in Manaus, Laurance and his colleagues developed comprehensive computer models that could examine the impact of the dozens of projected highways, waterways and other infrastructure projects. They came to the alarming conclusion that if the schemes were fully implemented, as much as 42 percent of Brazil's Amazon basin would be destroyed or seriously damaged by 2020.

As has been shown time and again in Amazonia during the past 40 years of development, it is the construction of roads that makes the biggest impact. It has been estimated that 80 percent of deforestation in Amazonia has occurred in a

30-mile (50-km) corridor flanking roads and highways. The road-building component of the Brazil on the Move project is therefore critical. As Laurance explained, "Historically, the Amazon has been nibbled away at the edges, but now what's been happening is like somebody going right in and chopping it up."

The STRI report did not take a strident antidevelopment line. It accepted that Brazil must encourage development of resources in the Amazon, but argued for less destructive methods of exploitation. "Rather than punching many new roads and highways into the remote frontier," Laurance said, "we are pushing for slower deforestation and more efficient use of existing agricultural lands than cattle ranching."

Very recently, cattle ranching has been joined by soybean production as a major factor in Amazonian agribusiness. This has come about because China at the end of the 20th century switched dramatically from being an exporter of soybean products to the world's biggest importer. Brazilian agribusiness was quick to exploit this shift and is now second only to the United States as an exporter of soybean products, and accounts for 24 percent of the world's production. "Soya farming really is emerging as the critical driver of Amazonian deforestation," according to Laurance. Ironically, Brazil's decision to produce only non-GM soya has only increased the pressure on the rain forest. Because of the fear of GM contamination from countries to the south of Brazil, growers of non-GM soybeans are continuously moving north, encroaching more and more on Amazonia.

The preservation of the rain forest and the role of ecotourism

Parts of Amazonia have been set aside as protected areas within a system of national parks and reserves. Unfortunately the degree of protection actually received is patchy, and sometimes nonexistent. The huge areas involved, the value of illegal trading in timber and animals and the limited resources that can be set aside for conservation make policing of this system almost impossible. If protecting biodiversity can be seen to improve the lives of the local people and the economy of the region, protection will improve. One idea has been to create so-called "extractive reserves" within Amazonia, where development can be practiced without devastation, by combining conservation with ecological balance and an improvement in the quality of life of the local peoples. Some activities that are already having some success are the extraction of rubber and the

Above: Exploring the forest and waterfalls near the town of Presidente Figueiredo.

Following pages: (Page 136) Tourists can take advantage of the many ferry and boat services on the Amazon which provide a relatively eco-friendly means of moving about this vast region. (Page 137) Tour companies, such as Adventure Amazon, are at the forefront of ecotourism in the area.

Above left and right: An important part of ecotourism is to engage visitors in a unique rain forest experience. The more people who know about the region and its unqiue inhabitants the better the chances for its survival into the future.

Opposite: Hotel de Selva on the spectacular Anavilhanas Archipelago.

cultivation of rice, manioc and corn. It is hoped that these sustainable activities will provide an income for people living in the forest and reduce the illegal extraction of forest hardwoods, as well as poaching.

At the opposite end of the scale is Jaú National Park. Established in 1986 to protect part of the Jaú River and its rich ecosystems, it is Brazil's largest national park at nearly 9,000 square miles (22,000 sq km) and in 2000 was given World Heritage Park status by UNESCO. About 16 hours from Manaus, it is one of the world's richest and most diverse environments. There are no visitor facilities and only 1,000 inhabitants in the whole park — a true wilderness region. Another approach has been taken with Mamirauá Reserve, 4,000 square miles (11,000 sq km) of rain forest between the Solimões and Japurá rivers. The reserve includes the largest intact area of floodplain in Brazilian Amazonia and a well-run ecotourism center. Set up in 1996, it is at the fore-

Opposite and left: A trip on one of the thousands of rivers and tributaries in Amazonia is often the best way to see the forest and wildlife.

Above: Meeting the locals at a tourist park.

Opposite: Chico Mendes Park is a memorial to an important activist who organized resistance against forest clearances in the state of Acre and promoted sustainable exploitation of the rain forest. The park includes theme huts which represent the different aspects of life in the region.

front of the sustainable development of reserves, combining conservation, research and ecotourism.

Tourism in Amazonia is a growth industry, and many think it offers at least a partial solution to the chronic dilemma — how to create prosperity in the region without destroying it in the process. Only part of Mamirauá Reserve is used for tourism because, conducted carelessly, tourism could be just one more nail in the rain forest's coffin. It is understandable that people who have spent a lot of money to get to such an exotic location are eager to see as much wildlife as they can, but restraint is called for. Off-road vehicles plunging through the wetlands erode the thin topsoil and scar the landscape. High-powered motorboats churn up tranquil waters, spread pollution and disturb the fauna (the endangered giant otter, for example, is sensitive to noisy intrusion; lactating females are easily put off their milk, which means starving cubs).

Properly monitored and conducted, however, tourism has much to offer Amazonia, and not only in terms of hard cash, important though that is. As more and more people from the prosperous nations come to see for themselves just how marvelous the Amazonian rain forest is, and how irreplaceable in its unequaled but delicate biodiversity, so the pressure will continue mounting to ensure its survival. At the same time, as tourism creates employment for increasing numbers of locals, so it reinforces the incentive to preserve what it is that the tourists are drawn to.

EPILOGUE

The Future: A Matter of Global Concern

Opposite and above: Aerial views of the Amazon flood plains.

As the third millennium gets underway the Amazon rain forest finds itself in the glare of a global spotlight. Everyone at least pays lip service to the importance of its continued existence, although those who continue to plunder it ruthlessly for short-term gain are ignorant or irresponsible or both. Brazen timber-cutting in protected areas is perhaps the most obvious case in point. The unspoken rationale here would seem to be that the rain forest is there to be ransacked, in the same way that everyone tacitly accepts that other nonrenewable resources such as coal and oil will continue to be exploited as long as they hold out. That mindset refuses to countenance such issues as biodiversity, indigenous peoples, the greenhouse effect or indeed anything at all that stands in the way of immediate profit.

Such concerns, too, mean little to the desperately poor who are focused on trying to keep body and soul together. Poverty is the root cause of the illegal trade in Amazonian wildlife. A report issued in Brazil toward the end of 2001 claimed that animal trafficking was the third most lucrative form of global smuggling, worth an esti-

Above: Macaws (left) and the woolly monkey (right) are just two of the many species of the rain forest suffering from the illegal international trade in endangered animals.

Opposite: The vastness of the rain forest, and its impact on the world's climate and biodiversity, mean that its future should be of concern to all.

mated $15 billion a year. It further claimed that nearly 40 percent of the wildlife — from butterflies to jaguars — came out of Brazil, with Belém the center of the trade. The poachers are for the most part too poor and hungry to have scruples about snaring a monkey here or a bird there, although in the nature of things it is not they who reap the colossal rewards. Collectors of rare species are said to pay up to $70,000 for a particularly rare macaw and more than $20,000 for one of the rarest of the tiny tamarins.

Ironically, the naked self-interest displayed by loggers, smugglers and others is reinforced by some of the more absurd nostrums peddled by those encamped on the wilder shores of the environmentalist lobby. They would like to see Amazonia returned to its pre-Columbian state of grace, where the indigenous peoples would once again roam the vast expanses of the rain forest alone, as if five centuries of history had never occurred — nature and nomadism good; modern industrial and post-industrial society bad. Rapacious loggers and the like are not alone in dismissing this for the nonsense it is. The nations of Amazonia are populous and growing fast. Economic and social needs exist here and now, not in some idealized past. The settlement of Amazonia cannot be reversed. Those who have put down roots there have to earn their living. However justified the criticisms of past and current exploitation practices, it flies in the face of rea-

Above left: Part of the town of Benjamin Constant — named for a nineteenth century Brazilian politican and philosopher — on the Javari River, a remote region on the Brazil-Peru border.
Above right: Clouds gather over rain forest in Pará.

son to suggest a self-denying ordinance on the use of natural resources *per se*. It is armchair environmentalism at its most self-indulgent, and if it has any effect at all it is to discredit the movement as a whole.

At the political level, all the governments responsible for Amazonia accept the need to balance economic interests with the need to preserve and conserve the rain forest. But not surprisingly they bridle when they find themselves on the receiving end of lectures by North Americans and Europeans (often under the cloak of international agencies such as the G-7 nations). They pointedly ask critics for their own national credentials over environmentalism. After all, North Americans and Europeans did not hesitate to exploit their own resources to the hilt in the course of creating their own successful economies. Quite the contrary. That is why the great primeval forests of Europe have all but vanished. That is why the modern United States bears so little resemblance to the pristine wilderness that greeted the early settlers. The charge of hypocrisy becomes if anything even more difficult to evade when it comes to the greenhouse effect and global warming, since the U.S. is notoriously the world's worst offender when it comes to pouring noxious gases into the atmosphere. From the perspective of those on the spot, it rings rather hollow for the rich to preach self-denial to the poor.

The need for sustainable development

If the wealthy nations are serious about helping Amazonia, they will have to lend practical support to measures aimed at achieving sustainable development. For that is the hope of the future. At a personal level, that implies at the very least a commitment not to support such activities as poaching and illegal logging by purchasing the end products. An earlier example may be instructive. Big cats such as tigers and leopards are highly endangered in the wild, but they would surely be extinct by now if opinion in the western world had not turned decisively against killing them for their skins during the second half of the 20th century.

There is widespread acceptance of the fact that, to date, attempts to exploit the region's natural resources have brought disappointing returns while incurring an unacceptable ecological cost. It is also widely accepted that sustainable development requires restraint — that there can never be golden eggs if the goose is allowed to perish. At the Earth Summit that took place, appropriately, in Rio de Janeiro in 1992, over 100 heads of government and thousands of lesser officials came together to discuss global environmental issues. Rio was dismissed by some as having been no more than a talking-shop, but even so it raised global awareness of the fragile state of the rain forest. It remains to be seen, however, if the wealthy nations will dig deep into their pockets to help fund the policies that are essential to sustainable development. If the rain forest is of such global significance, it requires a global response.

There are encouraging signs that new logging, reforestation and cultivation methods are increasing yields while reducing destruction. Well-regulated ecotourism, which is growing and will continue to do so as long as the rain forest remains intact, is another way to boost the economy without destruction.

At the same time the pharmaceutical potential of rain forest products remains

Above: A strip of forest follows the banks of a stream across a sea of cleared farmland.

149

Above left: Cavern and waterfall near the town of Presidente Figueiredo.
Above right: Marájo Island.

Opposite: The lush green canopy of the rain forest, broken only by a river channel, is a magnificent sight that must be preserved for the future.
Following pages: Yanomami children.

incalculable, and represents a very good example of sustainable development. The medicinal powers of several vegetable species found in the Amazonian forest are indisputable. For over 40 years scientists have known about the medicinal importance of plants such as guaraná and curare, essentials of the primitive culture of the region.

At the beginning of the 21st century Brazil is setting out to make a systematic assessment of the untapped potential of its medicinal plant species (which are to date innumerable, as their potential is unknown). An environmental agency has cataloged some 300 medicinal plant species, but it is confidently believed that this represents only a tiny fraction of what is in this natural medical cabinet. The Brazilian authorities are extremely anxious to stamp out "bio-piracy," whereby Amerindian tribes are bribed or coerced into providing plant remedies for illegal export. In the long run, potentially billions are at stake.

Economic incentives of this sort will play an essential role. For in the long run, the remaining rain forest can only be preserved if those in possession of it accept unequivocally that it is in their vital interests to see that it does.

Glossary

Alfândega Custom house.

Boto River dolphin.

Caboclos Backwoodsmen, subsistence farmers and fishermen.

Campesinos Small farmers.

Fazenda Ranch or large farm.

Friagem Cold fronts coming up from Antarctica bringing a sharp drop in temperature to parts of Amazonia.

Garimpeiros Wildcat gold miners.

Igapó Floodplains of "black-water rivers," in which the water although sediment-free has been stained by dissolved organic matter.

Jacarés açu Black caiman.

Kwarúp Ceremony to honor the recently deceased.

Manioc Root vegetable, usually pounded to a coarse flour.

Mercado municipal City market.

Onça pintada Jaguar.

Pajé Tribal healer.

Palmito The edible heart of the açai palm.

Peixe boi Amazonian manatee.

Pororoca Tidal bore.

Potoo A nocturnal bird with a mournful call.

Shabono A large communal hut some 25 feet (8 m) high with a large central opening.

Surazo Cold fronts coming up from Antarctica bringing a sharp drop in temperature to parts of Amazonia.

Terra firme Land that is never flooded by the Amazon River.

Várzea Floodplains of "white-water rivers," in which the water is an opaque muddy yellow or brown color due to undissolved sediments.

Selected bibliography and further reading

Atlas do Meio Ambiente do Brasil. Serviço de Produção de Informação, Ed. Terranova, Empresa Brasileira de Pesquisas Agropecuárias — Embrapa, Brasília, 1994.

Beozzo, J.O. *Leis e regimentos das missões. Política indigenista no Brasil.* Ed. Loyola, São Paulo, 1983.

Bierregaard, Richard O. Jr. *Lessons from Amazonia: The Ecology & Conservation of a Fragmented Forest.* Yale University Press, New Haven and London, 2001.

Boff, Leonardo. *O Casamento entre o céu e a terra.* Ed. Salamandra, Rio de Janeiro, 2001.

Capobianco, Paulo, Adalberto Veríssimo, Adriana Moreira, Donald Sawyer, Iza dos Santos and Luiz Paulo Pinto. *Biodiversidade na Amazônia Brasileira: Avaliação e ações prioritárias para a conservação, uso sustentável e repartição de benefícios.* Ed. Estação Liberdade e Instituto Socioambiental, São Paulo, 2001.

da Fonseca, Gustavi A.B., Anthony B. Rylands, Cláudia M. R. Costa, Ricardo B. Machado, Yuri L. R. Leite. *Livro Vermelho dos mamíferos ameaçados de extinção.* Fundação Biodiversitas, Belo Horizonte, 1994.

Dorson, Mercedes and Jeanne Wilmot Carter. *Tales from the Rain Forest: Myths and Legends from the Amazonian Indians of Brazil.* Harper Collins/Ecco Press, New York, 1997.

Good Kenneth and David Chanoff. *Into the Heart: One Man's Pursuit of Love and Knowledge Among the Yanomami.* Longman, London, 1996.

Goulding, Michael et al. *The Smithsonian Atlas of the Amazon.* Smithsonian Institution Press, Washington, 2003.

Harris, Roger and Peter Hutchinson. *The Amazon: A Guide to the River and its Region.* Bradt Publications, Bucks. UK, 1998.

Little, Paul E. *Amazonia: Territorial Stuggles on Perennial Frontiers.* Johns Hopkins University Press, Baltimore, 2001.

Magalhães, A.C. *Sociedades indígenas e transformações ambientais.* Universidade Federal do Pará, Belém, 1993.

Noble, John, Andrew Draffen, Robyn Jones, Chris McAsey, Leonardo Pinheiro. *Brazil.* Lonely Planet Publications, Melbourne, 2002.

Pearson, David L. et al. *Brazil — Amazon and Pantanal.* Academic Press, London, 2001.

Rizzini, Carlos Toledo, Adelmar F. Coimbra Filho e Antonio Houaiss. *Ecossistemas.* Ed. Index, Rio De Janeiro, 1991.

Robinson, Alec. *Amazon.* Cadogan Books PLC, London, 2000.

Smith, Nigel H. *The Amazon River Forest: A Natural History of Plants, Animals and People.* Oxford University Press, Oxford, 1999.

Webb, Alex. *Amazon: From the Floodplains to the Clouds.* Monacelli Press, New York, 1997.

Wood, Charles H. and Roberto Porro (editors). *Deforestation and Land Use in the Amazon.* University Press of Florida, Gainesville, 2002.

Websites

www.amanakaa.org

www.amazonia.org.br

www.amazonlife.com

www.amazonrivers.org/riverlinks.htm

Conselho Indigenista Missionário www.cimi.org.br

www.extremescience.com/AmazonRiver.htm

Fundação Nacional do Índio www.funai.gov.br

Instituto Brasileiro do Meio Ambiente e dos Recursos Naturais Renováveis www.ibama.gov.br

Instituto Nacional de Pesquisas na Amazônia www.inpa.gov.br

Instituto de Pesquisa Ambiental da Amazônia www.ipam.org.br

Instituto Socioambiental www.socioambiental.org

www.nationalgeographic.com/wildworld/amazonriver/

World Wildlife Fund for Nature, Brasil www.wwf.org.br

www.worldwildlife.org/amazon/

Photographic credits

Index

Opposite: Houses in the town of Benjamin Constant on the Javari River.